the boys of indy

the boys of indy

by PHIL BERGER and
LARRY BORTSTEIN

Corwin Books / New York

Published by
CORWIN BOOKS
275 Madison Avenue
New York, N.Y. 10016

Designed by Soho Studio

The authors would like to thank Donald Davidson of the United States Auto Club and Hal Higdon for their aid and support.

Courtesy of John Mahoney

contents

introduction

In the hoopla that surrounds the annual Indy 500 race, the men who make the event possible sometime become secondary to the purposes of the pageant. There are exceptions, the handful of leading drivers whose names are known even far from the Indianapolis metropolis. The rest, though, are overshadowed by the focus on automotive refinements and speed, the redhot themes of any Indy year.

Which is a shame. For the stories of all the drivers who drive the Indy 500 are worth the telling, no matter whether they are winners or also-rans. To get to Indy is an obsession. And in the cause of that obsession, the drivers travel some strange roads.

The cost of being an Indy driver is like the speeds at which they race, often excessive. It is a sport where broken bones can be a blessing, given the more grisly option that a crash can impose. *That* cost is the obvious one. There are more, though.

For some Indy aspirants, the cost is, quite simply, in cash dollars. Starting out, a racer intent on moving up to the bigtime can invest his own hard-earned wages. Not a few reach rock bottom, acquiring competitive racing machines early in their careers.

It is not only the money that they invest. The time expended goes beyond race day. The car is forever being tinkered with. The hours before the race are considered crucial in getting results from a balky machine. The clock is hard on a driver during the weeks and the days before a race. Some solve the problem and save a few working hours by sleeping in their garages.

That kind of monastic dedication can undermine the other lives the drivers lead away from the track. It's another cost the sport imposes. Marriages sometimes come apart from the long hours. Personal lives suffer.

Yet some say it's worth it. The Grand Prix racer, Phil Hill, once put it this way to writer Pat Jordan: ". . . It's an outlet for people whose lives and selves were inadequate. They try to put order and meaning into their lives by imposing their will on something potentially chaotic. A racer believes he makes his deadly machine safe. He plays God. He is one of the Blessed. His sport *must* be deadly so that in competing and surviving his skill takes on mystical qualities."

So there is magic in the race. And there is gray routine. There are all shades of emotion and all sorts of characters. The men who drive Indy are preachers, farmboys, self-made magnates, college grads, high school dropouts—each one of them with a racing experience that is uniquely his. **In this book, and in their own words, the drivers tell about it. They are The Boys of Indy.**

the boys of indy

jerry karl

JERRY KARL'S battle to get to Indy
cost him broken bones and hard times.
But he persisted and got what he wanted—
a ride in the five-hundred-mile classic.

Nineteen sixty-seven was a hard winter. Months before I'd broken both collarbones in a race. Other winters I'd worked hard labor. Part-time jobs. Earn enough 'til it was time to go racing again.

'Sixty-seven, though, it was impossible. Both collarbones were broken, the muscles and ligaments were all torn. I couldn't even lift my arms above the shoulder. We had a baby, and what little money we had went to feed him. There was practically no food. It was so bad you won't believe what I did.

I couldn't shoot a shotgun because of the injury. What I did, I'd tie a board to the front bumper of my car and go out on the Jones Beach Causeway. And just about dusk the grass by the highway would be loaded with rabbits. And rabbits—when they see lights—they stand and stare at 'em. So I tied this bumper about six or seven inches above the ground. And drove down the grass along the causeway for a mile, turned around and came back and picked all the rabbits up and put 'em in the trunk.

We just didn't live very good back then. One thing about racing: You can't race and hold a steady job. There's no way, unless you happen to be fortunate enough to come from money.

Whatever money I had, I put back into my car. No matter what I was driving—stock car, midget, sprint—the money was used to make that car go faster. Most of what I owned was what we call *junkers*, mediocre cars. You had to keep tinkering with it to get a few miles per hour more from it. It was an education driving those crates.

Some of the money came from racing. And not all of it was your official sanctioned kind. Hell, I remember when I was seventeen, eighteen years old and living in Valley Stream, Long Island. There was a rich kid name of Harvey from Lynbrook who hired me for street racing. He had a fire-engine-red Cadillac with a full racing engine in it. Harvey liked owning it and driving it. But he wasn't too fired up about racing it.

The races would be out on Cross Bay Boulevard, one exit west of JFK Airport. And the racing crowd those days hung around a place called the Bow Wow, sort of like a Nathan's. And matches were set up there. Man to man. For money. Harvey got me to run the Caddy for him.

A lot of times what they'd do—it'd be late at night—they would block traffic. Put two cars across the road like sawhorses. And off we'd go. Usually half a mile, three-quarters of a mile. A preset distance. Winner kept the money. And whatever Harvey won, he'd throw me twenty-five, thirty dollars for the race.

Those early days I'd make money any way I could. At one time my brother-in-law and I had a pickup truck. And with it we'd manage to turn a buck. We'd go around, checking the roofs of houses in places like Hewlett and Baldwin. And when we'd see shingles missing, we'd go up, ring the bell, and offer to repair the roof for twenty-five, fifty dollars.

Another source was a scrap-metal yard in Oceanside. This yard worked mainly with plants and factories and aircraft industries. And when they got junk mixed together—like stainless steel and aluminum and regular steel—they'd just throw it in a pile outside the fenced-in main area. To them it was just penny-ante stuff they didn't want to be bothered with. They made their money on stuff that came separated. They could just press it and bundle it.

To us, though, with a little bit of sorting through, it was a payday. In a couple of hours we could have maybe fifty dollars worth of stainless steel. And for six months we sorted through it. They saw us but figured we were just taking a few pieces for personal use. And that didn't bother them. When they realized we were in it for a profit, they ran us off.

One time an eccentric old man, very wealthy, died in Rockville Centre. This guy and his brother owned a few weird little race cars. Anyway, a few years before the old man died, he'd gotten married. And for some reason, this had set him and his brother to quarreling. Which, it turned out, was to our advantage.

What made us stop at the widow's door was we saw some scrap metal in the yard. It turned out, though, the good stuff was inside. She said to us, "Would you be interested in some machinery?" She took us to the basement. Her late husband had everything a guy like me could dream of. Welding equipment, lathes, drill presses, milling machines, brakes, everything. Plus bins of scrap metal, copper, stainless, and so on.

She wanted to get as much money out of it before the brother came around and confiscated it. What we did, we'd buy a load of, say, copper and go out and sell it for forty cents a pound. Then, with our profit, we'd buy more material from her until we cleaned the place out. As for the equipment: The duplicate pieces we sold, the rest I set up shop with in my garage. It was a very lucky day. With the machinery, I had a nice shop. And the extra money gave us the funds to do a nice job on the three-quarter midget I was building then. With it, we won the first race we entered and later the T-Q championship.

Once my collarbones mended [1968], I decided to take aim at USAC [United States Auto Club] racing. That's the circuit that Indy cars (also known as "championship cars") race on. (USAC also organized sprint, midget, and stock-car circuits.) USAC was the big leagues. Up 'til then I'd paid my dues in the minor circuit, the small obscure tracks. Now, though, I felt I was ready for USAC sprint races as a jumping point to Indy. It didn't take long before I began to wonder, though.

As usual, the car I had was a junker. In USAC sprint racing the guys in it are fairly wealthy, and they have a lot of everything. They come to the races with a trailerload of wheels and tires so they can really get the right combinations for gripping the track. They have real sharp engines and a lotta suspension parts and springs so they can get the chasses just right.

Another thing in USAC racing: You don't have a whole lot of time. You get about a five-minute warm-up session, and you gotta be ready to qualify for the race. So in that five minutes you have to assess your race car—"sort it out," we say—and figure what changes to make to qualify. Things like whether to change tires or gear ratios.

Familiarity with the tracks helps, naturally. Lack of it cost me in my second race. The place was Eldora Speedway in Rossburg, Ohio. I drew a late qualification number. In dirt-track racing, the track changes considerably all through the program as it's being used. And it was drying out very fast. So a guy come up to me. Supposedly, he knew the race track. He said that by the time I tried to qualify, the track would be dried out and the tires I had on would be wrong for it.

I listened to him and changed the tires. So what happened? I ended up spinning three hundred sixty degrees on the first lap. The time it cost me was crucial. I missed making the race by one-hundredth of a second.

It wasn't the only problem I had. I'd figured to earn money by making the race, enough to get me to the next race, which was in Winchester, Indiana. There was a week layover. Again, I was just about broke.

My brother-in-law and I headed toward Winchester. On the way we heard that a factory had blown up in Richmond, Indiana. A big explosion. A disaster—many people killed. We figured we could get a job there, helping clean up the debris. There was no way, though. It was all volunteers. Which was fine. But we were into making some money. We *had* to make some money.

We continued on to Indianapolis. No luck there. Not even for the day-job outfits—Manpower, places like that. We drove to the Indianapolis Speedway. Tried to get a job painting chairs or something. But they hired only those who signed on to work through the month of May. No day-by-day work.

Things got worse. The Winchester race was rained out. So now, we faced another week with no prospect of money.

We tried to sell our blood. But they had all the blood they needed from volunteers because of the explosion in Richmond.

So we said, "Hell, let's pack it up and go back. At least long enough to go back and make a few dollars. Then we can try again." I have to admit, though, I was beginning *Jerry* to wonder if I was kidding myself about being an Indy *Karl* driver. The dream was wearing thin.

8

I'd had that dream for a long time. Growing up in Valley Stream, Long Island, cars were my obsession. As a little kid, I hung around the gas station. My dad objected. The more he objected, the more I wanted to do it. My dad at that time worked on Wall Street. He was a coffee broker. And I guess he had big ideas for me. And they didn't involve hanging around gas stations.

One thing my dad didn't know was that back in the seventh, eighth grade I had a car. I was twelve years old then. It was a 1936 Ford, cream-colored, that another fellow and I bought from an older kid for fifteen, twenty dollars. I kept it at the other kid's house. Took it apart and pulled the engine all apart. When we first got it there, we used to back it up and down the driveway. That's as far as we got.

Had a motorcycle when I was thirteen. I don't understand how these things were sold to me because I was so young. But they were. Fella had this Indian Chief sitting there at the gas station for sale. And I bought it from him for thirty-five dollars. Wish I had it today. Worth quite a bit of money. But an Indian Chief—that's a big motorcycle. That's the biggest bike Indian made. And they were used for police bikes in those days.

And I'd never ridden a motorcycle before. I never rode anything but a bicycle. And this guy that sold it to me says, "Can you ride that?" And I said, "Sure I can ride it." And he's looking kind of funny at me.

Well, I'm full of confidence. I'd been sitting on it a hundred times, making believe I was running it, you know.

I'd just go over there and sit on the motorcycle. So anyway, I get it all paid off, and I'm ready to go. And I can't get it started because I'm not heavy enough to kick it over. So he started it for me.

And I put the clutch in and put it in first gear, and somehow or other I got it moving. And a motorcycle isn't hard to ride once you get it moving. As long as you keep it going fast enough, it's not going to fall over. So I took off out of the gas station and I rode it in first gear—like 10, 15 miles an hour—'til I got a couple blocks away. Then I got going, and I tried to shift it.

An Indian is a three-speed tank shift. And they were kind of strange 'cause first was all the way forward, and then there was neutral, then there was second, and then there was like another neutral, and then third. And you could get neutral in between both gears. So I shifted it from first to second. And when I went from first to second, I went into neutral. And I pulled it back and it went past second into the other neutral. Meanwhile, the bike is slowing down, see, getting slower and slower. Finally, I couldn't get it into gear, and it fell over on me.

And it's on top of my leg. I can't get up, see. And the motorcycle's still running, *pup-pup-pup*. And this guy comes around the corner. And I remember . . . it was an old man and a woman. And the woman was driving the car, and she stops and looks over. And she says to me, "You all right?" And I never did get a chance to answer. This man with her looks over and says, "Sure, he's all right. Those motorcycle guys are tough. C'mon honey, let's go." [Laughs.] And they left me lying there with the motorcycle on top of me.

Anyway, I kept the Indian Chief on a farm belonging to a friend of mine. I got pretty good with it. But I decided I wanted to go out on the street. Well, picture this motorcycle. I had fallen on it a hundred times. The lights were all busted off. It was just a wreck. This friend of mine and I made up a cardboard license plate. And put it on. And took off down the street with it.

Two little kids on this big hawg. So we come up to a

traffic light. And there was a cop there directing traffic. You know, we had to wait in line. And he saw us. He came up to us. I said, "Hang on, Bobby!" And I took off. And I cut through this parking lot. Thirteen, fourteen years old. We're hot dogs, right. We lost this cop.

Same thing happened a few days later by a synagogue. There was a cop there, and he was directing traffic. We get up like three or four cars behind. And he sees us. And he's looking at us. He lets the cars go by. And we come up. I'm going real slow. He puts his hand up. I say, "Hang on, Bob!" I rev it up, pop the clutch and it stalls. The jig was up. He had me follow him to my home. That's how Dad found out I was still screwing around with things that moved.

I was a wild kid. Did a lot of joyriding. I had a ticket for driving without a license before I was old enough to have a license. In those days, there was a car-wrecking yard run by a guy named Mo. He used to have cars that he'd get in there that were junk, and he'd take an engine out of one, this and that out of another. And guys he had working for him would piece together cars. He always had three or four running cars to sell. And he had a trailer there. And the keys to the cars were in the trailer. So we used to sneak in there at night, get the keys, and drive those cars around the dirt road he'd made in the yard.

And I guess he caught on to what we were doing. He knew his cars were being driven. And they laid for us one night. A bunch of 'em. And they caught us. And did Mo ever give me a good whipping. Knocked the stuffing out of me. And that cured me of going to Mo's junkyard to drive his cars.

But I came back there—oh, I guess it must have been a month later—to buy some parts, and he remembered me. And we got to talking. I had done street racing—in fact, I was notorious for it. But I'd never thought of organized racing. Mo was a big racing fan. Especially dirt cars. And he began to take me to the races. Out to Freeport, Long Island. And pretty soon I was doing it myself, with Mo's help.

A kid whose father owned the gas station had what they called a novice stock car, which he used to run at Freeport. It was a 1950 Ford, completely stocked with roll bars. This kid tried racing it and didn't like it. So I bought it from him for fifty or seventy-five dollars and worked on it at Mo's junkyard.

Eventually, I started racing it at Freeport. At that time I was fifteen years old. I raced as Jerry Karl, but I falsified all the papers. Birth certificate, written permission from my parents, and so on. Right off, though, I won a ton of races.

Of course, Mo helped me. We doctored the car some. What they'd do at Freeport was, they'd check the car after the race to make sure it was stock as far as shock absorbers and springs and tires were concerned. But what I used to do was take the right rear shock apart and weld it solid, its full length, and put it back on. And though everything looked right, the right side of the car was frozen solid. Against the sloppy springs in other cars it was an advantage.

Anyway. One night my father happened to go to Freeport to watch the races with a bunch of his cronies. He's sitting there, and he hears them announce my name. He came back to the pit area looking for me. When he saw it was me, though, he wasn't too angry. I guess he figured I had it in my blood to race cars.

But as I drove back east in '68, I was beginning to wonder about Indy racing. The way things went, I quit USAC racing in '68 and tried my luck again on the small circuits. Sprint cars, midget cars. Toward the end of the '69 season I'd made a name for myself around Hershey, Pennsylvania, running midget cars. The circuit I ran had a working arrangement with USAC. I applied for a USAC championship license. Not for sprint but championship cars, the kind they race at Indy.

My license depended on how I performed in three events. Based on those races USAC would decide whether to issue me a full license or advise me to get more experience.

The last three races of the year on the USAC championship-car circuit were Dover, Trenton, and Phoenix. At Dover I ran tenth. A two-hundred-mile race. My first championship race, and I made some points. I was thrilled.

At Trenton, though, the car broke down three-quarters through the race. About then I got into a squabble with two of the investors in the car. They thought I was doing the wrong thing with the money and wanted to take over the race car. Well, I knew that couldn't be done. If they took the car back to New York, there would be nobody to do the mechanical work on the car. At the time, I was living where I do now, in Manchester, Pennsylvania, and was taking care of the car. A normal mechanic can't do the mechanical work on the race car. He hasn't the knowledge. Also, a race car runs very fast, and it's gotta be right or somebody can get hurt. So I was thoroughly against letting them take the car.

Big squabble. And the car got "parked." I didn't get to run Phoenix. After negotiating I dug up a couple of new guys, and we bought off the others. I started to get ready for 1970.

All I needed was one more race. And if they gave me a full license, then I was allowed to go to Indianapolis and take my driver's test. Well, I knew the junker I had would never last out an Indy 500, but I figured at least it'd get me through the driver's test. First, though, I raced at Phoenix and Trenton and was awarded a full license. Then I went to the Indianapolis Speedway.

The driver's test was in four phases. I figured once I passed the test, maybe there was a possibility of getting somebody's backup car on the last day of qualifications. Just as long as I passed the test. Well, it didn't work out.

I got through the first three phases of the test. And then came the fourth and final phase. I ran three laps and blew the engine. That was the start of the most frustrating month in my life. I couldn't get me an engine to last me seven more laps. That's all I needed to pass my test.

Through the first three phases, there are just track observers to check you. The fourth phase is judged by veteran drivers, the drivers I'd have to race with. Well, five times they called the drivers out. And five times my engine blew. I couldn't make those seven laps.

In 1971 I didn't have the money to bring the car to Indy. There was a one-thousand-dollar entry fee. Then in '72 I heard of an Indy car that was half wrecked and might be put together. There was a bunch of junky Offy engines with it. Car and engines went for about ten thousand dollars.

I went to Carl Gehlhausen, who was in aluminum siding in Jasper, Indiana, and talked to him about putting the money up for the car. I had driven for him before. I said I'd work with his mechanic to straighten the car out and get to Indianapolis. And we got to Indy.

We were running 173, 174 miles per hour with that thing. But we had junk motors. And Carl didn't have thirty thousand dollars to go buy a new one. And it was forever blowing. We'd piece them together. They'd blow. And though we were going fast, we couldn't go fast long. So when it came to qualifying, I made three attempts in '72 to get into the race. And although we were fast enough, we couldn't complete the run all three times.

See, qualifying is an average speed of four laps. Doesn't matter if you break the track record the first three laps; if you don't finish the fourth, you're history. And I ran three laps at 173 miles per hour and blew on the fourth.

I couldn't believe I'd missed again. I was in shock. I *knew* I belonged in that damn race. And I just walked around. Like, I was numb. I watched the race. I'll never forget it. After that race was over, I went up in those grandstands. The crowd was gone. The stands were empty. I just sat there and cried my eyes out. I just fell apart.

Later on that year things started to break for me. At Pocono the race got canceled for two weeks because of the big flood they had. And it turned out that the guy who was to drive John Martin's backup car didn't come back. So I got to race that car. It was my first five-hundred-mile race.

I ran only twenty laps at Pocono and went out with a split fuel tank. But John called me and said how 'bout trying the California 500 at Ontario [California] Motor Speedway.

The problem was the usual one—money. I'd about run out again. I had this Ford station wagon, and I took off from Pocono in it and went to Milwaukee. There was a race in Milwaukee. I figured I might be able to get a ride. There was no ride. So I'm just about broke in Milwaukee, and I called Clint Brawner, who's a leading mechanic.

Brawner was in Phoenix. And I called him to ask for a ride. 'Cause I knew he had two cars. He said he couldn't promise me a ride. But if I was in trouble, I could come out there and work for him for a week. Because practice for the California 500 didn't start for another week.

When I arrived in Phoenix, I remember I had a dollar fifty in my pocket. So I went to work for Clint. He paid me one hundred or one hundred fifty dollars a week, plus put me up and fed me.

In California I was in John Martin's backup car. By day I was doing well in practice with it. Nights I was sleeping in back of my station wagon and eating at McDonald's. And just barely getting by. Then the day before qualifications I went out with Martin's car, and I blew the engine. That was it. Martin had one other engine, and that was in the car *he* was driving. So my car got parked.

Well, I'm sitting in California with no ride. I'm sitting on the pit wall, and a guy from Firestone asks me what's wrong. Told him I had no ride. He told me I should see Smokey Yunick. Smokey had just fired his driver. The guy offered to do the introductions. I met Smokey, and Smokey said he hadn't decided what he was going to do.

So I go to the coffee shop, and waited for him to make up his mind. I figured, though, it's never going to happen. But here comes Smokey through the door. Says, "Hey, you wanna run that thing?" Smokey had a Chevrolet-powered car. Experts considered it was an impossibility to put a stock block in the race since turbochargers had come into existence. But Smokey did it.

So I went out and ran it. And it turned out my first lap was 2 miles an hour faster than what the driver he'd fired had been doing. That driver had been running the car all month. And my third lap was about 5 miles an hour faster. But I didn't know this at the time. I had no idea. Smokey doesn't put the speeds up on a board like some others do. He just uses a stopwatch.

Well, one of the blowers exploded, and I shut it down and brought the car in. And I told him what happened. He said to me: "Which one blew?" And I didn't know which one. All I know is a blower let go. But I don't know which one. I didn't remember.

I get out of the car. He doesn't say another word to me. He pushes the car back to the garage. He left me standing there. Now I don't know from nothing, right? So I waited a few minutes, and I followed him back to the garage. And they're down there pulling the plugs out and the blower off and working like hell. I asked, "What do you think happened?" He just ignored me. Or I thought he did. No matter what I said, he wouldn't even acknowledge I was standing there, right?

And I figure: Oh damn, I must've really blown it. I couldn't understand what I did wrong, except I didn't know what blower let go. Anyway, I finally left the garage. I'm sitting over in the coffee shop, and I'm kind of depressed. I'm trying to figure out what happened.

Bob Harkey comes in. He's a fellow driver. I told him I thought I'd blown it with Smokey—he wouldn't even acknowledge me. He says, "Wait a minute. Was he looking at you when you were talking to him?" I said, "No. He was down working on the car." He said, "Don't you know Smokey's partially deaf?" I thought he was joking. He said, "Seriously, Jerry." At that time Smokey had partial hearing. He's since had it fixed.

Harkey said, "Go 'head back there and make sure he's looking at you when you talk to him." I said, "Okay, it's worth a try. But if you're putting me on, you better not be here when I get back."

So I went back to the garage. And now Smokey's back

by the bench. He has the blower off, working on it. Then he sees me come through the door, says, "I'll have this fixed in about an hour, and you can give it another try." I mean, I just felt about ten feet tall.

I qualified the car eighth fastest, but had transmission trouble with the car in the race and went out on the forty-fifth lap. I was credited with twenty-ninth place. But Smokey must have liked the job I did because the next year at Indy [1973], I was sitting among the pack in his Oriente Express. I'd finally made it.

Jerry
Karl

17

al unser

**AL UNSER is part of a renowned racing family.
From Pikes Peak to the Indy oval,
Al and the Unsers have been there.**

Everybody in racing knows about the Albuquerque Unsers. In one way or another our family has been in racing since way back in the 1920s when my father, whose name was Jerry, started riding motorcycles with his brothers Louie and Joe in Colorado City, Colorado. Now they call that town Colorado Springs. Pikes Peak is located there, and for years our family has just about owned that mountain, as far as racing is concerned. Especially Bobby, who won lots of races. Now his oldest boy, Bobby Junior is racing Pikes Peak. To race on Pikes Peak you go up the mountain about 60 miles an hour—only one car can be in any one space at one particular time. There's no room for riding two abreast or anything like that. People who think the kind of racing that goes on at Indianapolis is tough ought to have a look at the Pikes Peak race once.

I don't think there's ever been a family like ours in racing. Bobby and I are the only brothers who've ever won Indianapolis, and we've each won it twice. The twins were the oldest, Jerry and Louie. They might have won Indy too with better luck. Jerry was killed at the Speedway in 1959. I think about him a lot still, but I think about him alive, not dying in that crash at Indy. Like all the rest of us he was doing what he wanted to do, and I'm sure if he'd survived, he'd have gone on doin' it. I feel bad that he wasn't around to see Bobby and me win at Indy, but I feel just as bad about our dad not having been around to see us either. He died a few years ago before Bobby and I made it big, and I know he would've been very proud of us.

Then there was Louie, who was Jerry's twin. He was my mechanic the first year I went to Indianapolis, 1965. He might've been a pretty good driver too, except he got multiple sclerosis in 1962. He wanted to stay in the business, though. So he became a mechanic. He was always the best mechanic of the four of us. He's got a shop in Santa Ana, California, where he makes engines for cars and mostly for boats. People come into his place, and he can sell them souped-up engines for their regular cars, or he can make 'em special engines if they want to go racing.

You know, out of all us Unsers, the one that was maybe best known was Mom, our mother. Her name was Mary, but everybody in racing called her Mom, and she really enjoyed the sport and all the people in it. She had a nice influence on the sport. She was a very strong lady. She supported our racing completely, even when we had accidents. She was always behind us.

Mom passed away of a heart attack the week before Christmas in 1975. She died in Bobby's arms in Albuquerque, New Mexico. It was funny. She'd just went and had a physical, and the doc said, "Gosh, Mom, you're in better shape than you've been in years." It was just a couple of weeks later she had a heart attack.

Mom was famous for her green chili recipe, and every year at Indy she'd whip up vats of the chili, and all the drivers and all the crews would dig in, and Mom would just love doing it for all the guys. In 1976 Bobby ran the chili party for all the guys, and we hope we don't have trouble with our cars so from now on we can keep on running those parties in honor of our mother. She was some strong lady, as I say. She was always the first to come around if things weren't goin' so good, and say our luck was gonna change and that we just had to keep on going.

She was probably unusual for the women in this sport. A lot of marriages break up in racing because the women aren't strong enough to handle it. I married Wanda when we were teen-agers, and we had a pretty good life for a few years. We had three kids, two girls and a boy, and now my boy, Al Junior, looks like he's gonna go into racing. He's been in go-carts for a few years already.

But Wanda and I broke up in 1971, and Bobby's into

his third marriage now. It's not the sport. Hell, there are no more divorces among the drivers than there are anywhere else. You look at the statistics, and you see that the racing doesn't cause divorces. I know lots of people who get divorces, but they're not in the public eye, so you don't hear about them.

No, I think it's that many of the women who are married to drivers become very relaxed. They take things too much for granted. I've always wondered what breaks up marriages in racing, and I think what it is, is that the women can't take the travel, they get to thinking they're not part of it and start looking elsewhere.

It's not just the successful drivers that have that problem. It could be just about anybody. Lots of the drivers have gotten divorces. But I just don't think the sport is that hard on family life. If the two of you will accept it. Half of the women won't accept it. You can see how many drivers have gotten divorces by looking in the book—the book USAC puts out every year that lists all the drivers and their records and things. A lot of the guys have their children's names listed, but no wife. So you can see where all these guys have gotten divorces.

After Wanda and I broke up, she left Albuquerque for a while. She's back here now, though, with the kids. They're all in high school, and I see the kids a lot. I get along real well with all of 'em. I like the fact they're in Albuquerque because it's such a great town. It's more cosmopolitan than it was when we were kids, but it's got everything I like. Bobby and I both have property up in Chama, in the mountains, and we go hunting and snowmobiling up there, and it's a great life. Being outdoors a lot keeps us in good shape for racing, you know. We hunt elk and deer, and hell, we'd never leave Albuquerque for anything. I wish I wasn't gone as much as I am now, with all the things I have to do. When you get to our level in racing, you're away twice as much doing nonracing things as you are just racing. I like to come back to Albuquerque just to relax in the mountains or be outdoors on my own. I'm not one for sitting inside watching TV or anything like that, but being in Albuquerque or in the mountains relaxes me.

There's a lot of stories about how all of us Unsers grew up, and hell, just about every damn one of 'em is true. None of us four boys was what you call quiet. We had a lot of fights and were always out there getting into some sort of battle or another. I was the baby—I'm five years younger than Bobby—so the other guys didn't always want to be bothered by the likes o' me. But I tagged along and everything, and they usually let me. I looked up to all three of my brothers and they usually treated me pretty good.

Al Unser

23

Each of us kids had a donkey. They had to tie me on mine because my legs were too small to put underneath the donkey's stomach, so Bobby or Louie would get some rope and tie it around my feet, and away we'd all go. Hell, we were funny. We'd go catchin' rattlesnakes. There were lots of 'em around our property in those days. We heard once on the radio we could sell rattlesnake venom for ten dollars an ounce or something like that. Our folks had moved down to Albuquerque from Colorado Springs because the automotive business was in Albuquerque, and we always thought we could make some easy extra money by gettin' us some rattlesnakes and draining the venom out of 'em.

We caught all the rattlesnakes we could, but we never sold a damn bit of venom to anybody. So finally we just let the snakes go. We never killed any. We turned 'em loose so we could just go catch 'em again.

After my brothers all went into racing, they didn't have much time for me because I was much younger and couldn't go racing. But later on, when I got interested in racing, Bobby helped me a lot. All the years we've been in racing together we've been pretty close. When Bobby first was getting started, you know, he had to work at it by himself so he could know where he was going in the sport. But later on, I would have to say, he was very helpful.

None of us cared much about going to school. None of

the four of us ever graduated from high school, but the folks never hassled us about it. They knew we wanted to go racing, and they let us go our own way. They were always real good about it.

Sunday night was race night in Albuquerque, and all of us'd go down to Albuquerque Speedway for the races. It was a little dirt track, but it was a good place to learn how to race. Bobby was a big winner there. Jerry too. And when I got started in 1957, that's where I started.

Bobby and I are both what you call "hard chargers." We drive the hell out of every race we're in. If you can't do that, you shouldn't be out on the track. This isn't a sport where you can take things easy. Not at the speeds we go. And I'm all for going even faster. Hell, we're out there driving as hard as we can no matter how fast the car goes. I worked just as hard when the cars were going only 150 miles an hour as I do now when the cars go over 200. It's the equipment that makes the car go faster, *and* the driver. You can stand on the gas only so much, but if the car isn't built to go any faster than it is, you're just not gonna go any faster.

The way I look at it, you can't let down for a second. You have to go hard, even when you feel you can't catch somebody. You never know when he's gonna break down and you'll be in a position to get up there. I've been up near the front in a lot of races.

Naturally, once I started getting going good in racing, I wanted to win Indianapolis. I'm real proud that I won Indy twice in a row, but I'd be prouder if I could win a third or a fourth—ten times even. I might have won three straight actually, since I think my ride in 1969 might have been one of the best I ever had at Indy.

That was the first year I rode for Parnelli Jones and Vel Miletich. I've been with them all these years, and we are great friends and we've been very successful in a lot of business things together. When I say successful, I don't mean I could quit racing tomorrow and have enough money for the rest of my life. No way. You know, one year I won around five hundred thousand dollars in purses, but my take was only about one-fourth of that. I'm not tremendously wealthy by any means. I like the money because if I see something I want, I can buy it. But I don't want much.

Anyway, we went to Indianapolis in 1969 with a real good car. On the first day of qualifying I was fooling around riding on my motorcycle—I always loved my motorcycles. I fell off and broke my left leg. I was out for five weeks. Naturally I missed the Indianapolis race, and Milwaukee, and I think one other race.

So maybe I would have won three straight Indy races if I hadn't fallen off that motorcycle. But that didn't stop me from riding anymore motorcycles. I still ride them at Indianapolis and whenever I feel like. I'm not gonna live in any glass house. I don't believe in that.

I kind of made up for not getting to the race in '69, anyway. 'Cause 1970 was a great year for us. I won Indianapolis and nine other races and just ran away with the USAC driving championship. I don't think anybody ever had a year like that in USAC. I mean, everything went right that year. *Everything.* The car was right. The mechanics. I was right. I was ready. You find that very seldom. I was almost unbeatable. All we had to do, it seemed, was get the car out on the track, and the next thing you knew we'd won another one. When something like that's happening to you, you don't ask questions like, Is it gonna end soon or not? You just don't ask anything. You just figure you'll keep on rolling and things'll take care of themselves.

I won the pole for Indianapolis in 1970, and then I went out and ran practically the whole race in the lead. That doesn't hardly ever happen. But that's the kind of year it was that year. After the race was over, I was just coasting around the track, and I remember thinking, "Jeez, I can't believe how easy it was."

The second one was a little tougher. We started from the fifth spot, but we got the lead late and hung in there for the checker. Everybody wanted to know if it was more of a thrill to win the second than the first, but hell, like I say, I'm happy to win always. The big difference for me was the first time I won I lost all sense of direction. I couldn't find Victory Lane afterward. The second time I knew just where to go.

There was a different twist involved in 1971 too. Like always, Mom was in the stands watching Bobby and me race. She always said she didn't care which one of us won a race as long as one of us got first and the other got second. In that 1971 race Bobby was in an accident. Mike Mosley lost a tire going into turn four and hit the wall. Bobby was comin' along right in back of Mosley, and he spun and hit the wall too. Mosley's car caught fire, and there was a big mess on the track. They finally had to pull Mosley out of his car and get him to the hospital with a broken leg and some burns. Bobby came out of it with only a headache. But, naturally, when I was drivin' along, I didn't know what was happening. I came into turn four a little while after the fire broke out in Mosley's car, and I knew Bobby had been in that mess. But on the next lap I saw him standing there and waving at me. Believe me, that was awful good to see.

As far as our racing against each other, I feel the same racing against Bobby as against any other driver.

It hasn't turned out that we've gone against each other too much as far as winning is concerned. The years I've won a lot of races Bobby wasn't winning too many. The years he's won big, my cars haven't been too reliable. Actually, since '71 I haven't done a whole lot at Indy. Our team's cars keep giving us trouble, so we haven't really even been contenders. That gets to you after a while, but you have to keep on goin'. I wasn't a celebrity for a long time before I won Indy, so when I became a celebrity, that was a whole new deal at that time. Winning teaches you how to win and how to lose. It gives you confidence, which helps you win and helps you handle losing.

But even if I haven't done so well at Indianapolis, I'm not throwing in the towel. Hell, no. I've done real well in lots of other races, and I've rode the dirt tracks and been in the USAC Formula 5,000 series, which they sponsor with the Sports Car Club of America, and I've won a whole lot of races. A lot of people who don't follow racing all year round think that the Indianapolis 500 is about the only race going. But there's lots of other things worth shootin' for too. And I keep very active in racing. I like it. There's nothing else I like more. And the way things go in this sport, I'm liable to come back to Indianapolis one of these years and win a third one there.

I'm racing as much or more than I ever did. A lot of guys think it's foolish to run the dirt tracks, because you can't make that much money even if you win. The only big-money dirt-track race is the Hoosier Hundred, which is run at the Indianapolis State Fairgrounds. The big prize there is about fifteen thousand dollars. Even A. J. Foyt shows up for that one. But look, it's not the money. We just like those dirt tracks, and I'm gonna keep on runnin' them.

I figure I have five strong years left as a driver. I have no idea when the day'll come that I'll want to get out of it. Bobby's forty-three, and he's still going good. Foyt's forty-three or so. Roger McCluskey's forty-five or forty-eight. Lloyd Ruby still runs every once in a while. He'd run all the time if there was a car owner who'd put up the money. He's still competitive.

I'm at an age when I might be considered in my prime. Everybody talks about his prime. But I don't think anybody ever knows when his prime is. I think what happens is one day you look back and say, "That was my prime." Look at Foyt. He's had so many primes it's unbelievable. So I can't really say if I'm in my prime, if my prime already passed me by, or if I'm still heading into it. You never do really know.

This may seem like an unnatural way of life to some, but it seems like the most natural thing to me. Sometimes I scare myself on the track when dangerous things happen, but it goes as fast as it comes. I've had some pretty rough crashes, but as long as you walk away from them, you laugh at them. I guess we all think it won't happen to us, if we think about it at all, which we try not to. I guess what would make me quit sooner than anything would be the first time I'd feel afraid going into a race. You can't drive scared and survive.

That's why these speeds don't bother me. When I see USAC and the Speedway trying to slow us up, I say I don't care. But I do care. But after 1973 all they want to do is slow us down. 1973 was a bad year, sure. It rained, and there were accidents, and they started and restarted the race three different days. Everybody in the press ran out of things to write about so they started writing about the people dying. One thing led to another, and it all became a big nightmare.

That's who I blame in this whole thing—the press. So USAC and the Speedway people had to do something to prove they were trying to correct everything. So they just tried to slow the cars down. But the people in the stands don't know how fast the cars are going unless you tell them. There's no way the naked eye can tell if a driver's goin' 160 or 200. At Michigan, where the track is a two-mile oval, we go 196, 200—something like that—and the people watching the races there can't tell if it's 215 or 180. So it's not the speeds that are the problem in the sport. It's people who don't know the sport coming in and telling everybody else what to do. I actually think some people'd be happy if we just rode around at 100 miles an hour. Then it wouldn't be a sport anymore. It would be just something anybody could do. That's one thing racing isn't —something anybody can do.

We know better than anybody whether we're going too fast. You know you're going goddamn way too fast when your brakes don't work and you crash or something. Nobody has to come in and tell us that.

To tell you the truth, all of us who are in racing now would probably be in it even if the cars were much slower. It's in our blood. Mom always used to say—this would be when we'd go riding into the mountains with snowmobiles or bikes or whatever, and naturally we'd start racing each other—she'd say, "You'd be racing even if all they let you use was wheelbarrows." She was right about that. I really think we would. And we'd drive 'em as hard as we drive our race cars. 'Cause that's the way we are, Bobby and me.

Up until Bobby won Indianapolis in '68, we used to tease each other about who would be the first to win the 500. Both of us always did think we'd make it some day. It wasn't just something we dreamed about. We just both knew we'd win Indianapolis. Then he won in '68, so he was first. I crashed on the first turn of the forty-first lap, so I had plenty of time to go back to the garage and change my clothes and then I went to Bobby's pit.

I didn't talk to anybody, and nobody tried to talk to me. I just sat on the pit wall and watched the race. It came down near the end, and Joe Leonard was leading in Andy Granatelli's STP turbine car, and Bobby was second. Bobby was definitely faster, but Leonard had a lead, and I didn't know if there'd be enough laps left for Bobby to catch him. I knew if Bobby could catch him, he'd win, but there were only a few laps left.

But Leonard had no luck. With only nine laps to go, his car stopped. Just gave out. They never could get it started again. What a hell of a way to lose the Indianapolis 500. Of course, after that happened, there was no way for Bobby to lose, and when he got to Victory Lane, I ran over and shook his hand, then got out of there because it gets so crowded and confusing down there. I liked it real well when I made it there after my two wins.

I told you about how I missed the 1969 Indy race when I fell off my motorcycle. If I had won that year, I would have had three straight Indy 500s. After I won in '70 and '71, I went for three straight in '72 and came in second to Mark Donohue. That was better than I bargained for because I only started nineteenth. Bobby won the pole, but he should have figured right then that he was done. Bobby was winning the pole in lots of races there for a couple of years, but it seemed that he wasn't doing much besides that. In that '72 race he lasted only thirty-one laps and got thirtieth place. That was probably the biggest disappointment he ever had as far as racing was concerned. His car that year, the Olsonite Eagle, was easily the fastest on the track. He qualified at more than 195 miles an hour, and the second fastest guy was 192 something. Three miles an hour difference between the first and second fastest is amazing. That might have been the only time in the whole history of Indianapolis when something like that happened.

You know, talk about marriages breaking up in racing and all that, Bobby was with this girl for three years when all of a sudden one day last fall [October 1976] he called up and said he was goin' off and marrying the gal. Just like that. On the spur of the moment. So off they went, and nobody was really too surprised. Bobby's got the full respect of his kids and Bobby Junior, his oldest, could turn out to be a pretty good driver one of these days himself. He's already raced the Pikes Peak race, and he's shown that he knows what he's doing. There'll be a few more Unsers in this business yet, with Bobby Junior, and my boy, Al Junior, coming up.

My oldest girl, Mary—she's named after my mother—is even talking about racing. Last fall in Phoenix she broke the female speed record at a miniature track they had there. I broke the record for men just before that. I'm not against Mary or any girl or woman who wants to try to race. I just don't happen to believe that a woman ever will stand a chance against men in the Indianapolis 500 or the other big races. They just don't have the strength to last the distance. But, who knows? Maybe in years to come the women will catch up and be as good as the men drivers. I don't think it'll happen, but I've been wrong about different things before, so this wouldn't be the first time.

All I know is, I'm not gonna worry about what anybody else is doing or what they're worryin' about. I'm gonna keep on working myself to do the best job I can. It took me a long time to make it to the top, and I want to stay there as long as I'm in the sport. Whatever you may do in this sport, you're a bum unless you keep on doing it. That's the pressure. It's a long way down, and you don't want to fall off. You don't ever want to hit bottom because it's no fun down there. That's what scares me, actually. Not dying. Losing.

Al
Unser

31

jan opperman

JAN OPPERMAN mixes motor racing with
a life devoted to Christ's teachings.
His interest in the gospel follows a
tumultuous period as a dropout.

I'm called racing's hippie, even though that word isn't heard too much anymore. Other people call me a Jesus freak, but I hate to see the word *freak* used after Jesus. Yeah, Christianity turns me on more than anything ever did, and I tried everything else. If you want to call me anything, call me a Jesus man. That'd be nice. Up in the mountains where I live with my wife and four kids, up in Noxon, Montana, I built a little church out of logs and stuff, and I conduct services. I'm a Minister of the Gospel, which may not mean much to you unless you're as into it as I am. But it means an awful lot to me.

I guess besides Christianity the biggest turn-on for me all my life has been living in the mountains. I moved back to the mountains a couple years ago after me and my family had lived in a place called Beaver Crossing, Nebraska, which was close to where a lot of my racing was going on. Beaver Crossing is maybe 35 miles outside of Lincoln, way out in the country. There's no mountains near there, but at least it was way out in the country.

But I always knew I'd be back in the mountains someday. I grew up in 'em and thought that was the best kind of life.

I was born on February 9, 1939, in Westwood Village, near Los Angeles, but my folks knew it was best to raise kids in the country, so we moved up to Idaho when I was little. My dad had moved around a lot as a kid. He had been a pro fighter, he had bummed around, and he had a good feel for all different kinds of environments. He had been in the mountains, up near where I'm at now, and he knew what he wanted for us.

We're all up here now. I put my folks up in a little cabin only about a mile and a half from where I live. His name's Jim and hers is June, but we used to call her Mops to tease her because she was always moppin' up stuff. I had a younger brother, Jay, two and a half years younger, who was killed in a racing crash a few years ago when he was twenty-eight. He would have been something had he lived.

Anyway, when I was little, my folks moved up to Bonner's Ferry in the Idaho Panhandle. My dad drove logging trucks, but he didn't always make out too good. He moved us across the Idaho border into Washington for a while. We lived near Mount Rainier, so we had the mountain life there, too.

When I was sixteen, my dad still wasn't makin' out too good, so we moved down to the San Francisco area. Boy, that was terrible, a terrible downfall from the mountains. My dad knew it, but he also realized he wasn't supportin' the family right, the way he wanted to, in Washington. So I don't blame him for movin' us. We were poor, always, when we lived in Idaho and Washington. We had to hunt and fish to keep meat on the table, and we kept a garden for vegetables.

But I loved the way we lived then, and I'm livin' that way now again. It's a spiritual kick. It gets you hooked up with the land. Bein' up there you can't believe how you can get blowed away by what the mountains do to you.

I finished high school in a place called Hayward, California, near Oakland. After I got out on my own, I moved further into the country, into the mountains down there, or the hills as they call 'em there. I stayed down there until I was twenty-six.

I got into motorcycle racing down there, and I also did a little amateur boxing. But for a long time I was really wrapped up in the hippie movement, which was big in the Bay Area. I didn't go to Haight-Ashbury, the section in San Francisco where mostly all the hippies hung out. I had some connections there, but I wanted to do things my own way. So I didn't go there much. That was too much of a freak show for me. Everybody would dress up freaky—so did I, lots of times—and all the kids would try to spook the older people by dressin' weird, acting weird, and talkin' weird. It was just kind of a game. They were just putting everybody on. I didn't want to go there because who wants to be in a game all their lives?

I know you want to know if I smoked pot and took drugs. Hell, yeah, I sure did. Smoked a lot of grass in those days. Those were the kind of kicks I needed and went after in those days. I don't need that kind of stuff anymore. But then I went through a whole stage. I guess I was always lookin' for something. I remember back in '60 just finally dropping out of everything, going up in the woods in California and turning on, trying to figure out what this is all about, who's running it, and what I was supposed to do.

Jan Opperman

36

There was almost no talk about religion in our house. I don't even know what faith we were supposed to observe. I tried all sorts of Eastern religious cults, but I didn't find what I was lookin' for until '69, when I met this farmer kid in Nebraska. He was so nice I decided to try to turn him on to dope. Instead he turned me on to Christianity. I listened to his way of life, and I thought that was neater. I've been with Jesus ever since.

As I got older, I really started looking into it, the Bible, I mean. That's how I got hooked—reading the Bible, studying it, praying, you know. The whole thing is a turn-on for me. The New Testament is the best part because these are New Testament times. People can relate what's happening in the world to the New Testament. Anytime I get a little shaky or something, I sit down and read from the Bible, and it straightens it out every time.

I don't quote stuff from the Bible. But there are lots of passages I like that I always tell people to read. Like the thirteenth chapter of Corinthians and the First Book of John. Those are love chapters. They're about love, and love is what the whole trip's about. That's what God is, is love. When someone's loving you and being nice to you and you're doing the same back, everything's nicer then than probably any other time in your life. God says that's what I am—nothing more, nothing less.

Some of that stuff is pretty heavy. The hippie movement flirted with some of that, we talked about it. Mainly we wanted to get away from the people who said, "For me to be cool, I've got to have two of something you only have one of." But when things turned bad in the hippie movement, there was lots of violence and hurting people, and that wasn't what it was supposed to be about. That's why Christianity is so much better. That's why it makes more sense.

Ever since I was a hippie, and after that a real strong Christian, I always looked a lot different than the other race drivers. I always wore my hair long and wore different kinds of clothes, and now I have a cross on both sides of my helmet and down the back of my racing uniform. I don't know if the public thinks I'm weird or not, and I don't much care. I'm pretty sure the other drivers don't think I'm weird or a fanatic or anything. At least nobody's ever said that to me. I don't push it on people. If a guy's not interested, that's it. I've gotten a couple other drivers to become real strong Christians along with me. Guys like Rich Leavell and Bobby Jones, guys I drive USAC sprint cars with.

Bobby Jones was involved in an accident with me in '76 that really showed me what God and love were all about. Maybe I'd be dead by now if it weren't for my feelings about these things.

This was the Hoosier Hundred dirt-track race at the Indiana State Fairgrounds. It was a bad crash, real bad. I had maybe only one bad accident before that, in '70 in Sacramento, California, when the front end of my super sprint car fell off at 140 miles an hour. The car spun down the backstretch and hit a wall, but I was okay. This time I wasn't.

I hit the wall and was thrown out of the car. Later on I found out from these two friends of mine who were at the scene that a doctor came over and checked my pulse and my heart and my breathing. I didn't have any. My face was all purple and black. I was really wiped out. All that happened to Bobby was he banged up his knee a little. But I was so bad that the doctor pronounced me dead right there.

But, see, my friends were there, and some other people came down to the third corner where I was, other drivers and people from the different crews. You know, racing people maybe have more love for one another than any other group of people. And when all these people came over to where I was and prayed for me and expressed their love for me, God saw this—and remember how I said God is love?—He saw this, and He brought me back. He saw the love that was all around me, and He brought me back to life. There's no question in my mind. You can't make me believe any different.

That's why I get confused sometimes when people wonder how a guy can be a race driver and also a Christian. How can you be in a violent sport? People ask me that a lot. Well, I'll agree this is dangerous, but we have such love for each other, we respect each other so much and all the time, that this is a very Christian-type thing.

I don't deny that I do this because there's good money to be made. But I was doin' it even before I was making any kind of money in it, because I loved it so much. There is joy in doing work you enjoy, the Bible says.

It was back in California when I began with the motorcycles, but my size—I weighed one hundred and eighty pounds—was a drag for motorcycle racing. I didn't do too good in it. I started driving midgets down in the San Francisco area. But guys there told me I couldn't stay there and do anything in racing. There just wasn't enough goin' on. No races and no money. They said I'd have to go East —east of California, actually, like into the Midwest, where there was a lot of sprint racing and a lot of dirt tracks.

That's when I got started in my "outlaw" racing. I started doing good, and I was able to make my own deals with tracks and promoters for appearance money and guarantees and things like that. I had no interest in getting into one of the organizations because I had heard all about 'em, how they expected you to wear a tie and act polite and all that, and I wasn't interested in all o' that. I just wanted to go racing.

Those little cars I was driving all those years could be the most dangerous machines anyone can race. They're smaller versions of the Indy cars, but with unlimited power—four hundred or five hundred horsepower, maybe —and they could go as fast on turns as they could on straights. Hell, if anyone thought I was a sissy because I wore my hair long or wore freaky clothes, all they had to do was look at what I was racin', and they'd know different.

Jay, my brother, got killed in one of those cars. It was in Knoxville, Iowa. I was in Pennsylvania, which was where I did lots of my racing at that time. This was around 1969, I figure. Kenny Weld, another racer, who lived near me, came over to tell me Jay had been killed after he heard it from the promoter, who didn't know our phone number. Kenny wasn't that close to either Jay or me, but it broke his heart to tell us. You know, it was another racer involved, part of that love thing we all have for each other.

I think Jay would have been a big winner if he had lived. But I know what killed him. There's a lot of kids like him. He was very fast—he was always faster than I was —and very quick and had tremendous ability and desire. And those are dangerous things to have until you get a lot of experience.

In the race that killed him he was going too fast, trying to pass somebody, a real fast guy, a very fast guy. Jay couldn't shut off and just sneak by people. He was so aggressive that he had to zoom past the other guy. So he was blazing past this guy just wide open, and that track was superfast. The other car broke the suspension as Jay went by. The other guy swerved in front of Jay, and when Jay hit the other guy's wheel, he just flipped over. He was dead immediately. One of the big lessons in racing is you go by people gently. It takes a while to learn that. Too bad Jay never got the chance.

I still wear an old floppy hat he gave me once. It's kind of a good luck thing with me—and it hides the fact that I'm mostly bald in front!

I'll tell you, that racing I did in Pennsylvania and in the Midwest when I was racing for myself was real tough racing. But I got a lot of good rigs from promoters and owners who wanted me to come to their shows, and I won a lot of races. I drove a lot for a guy named Bill Smith, who owned a place called Speedway Motors in Lincoln. That's when I was living in Beaver Crossing. He and I got along real well, and we won some races together. I raced his cars in Iowa and Nebraska and Illinois, mostly.

But I also went to Pennsylvania a lot, especially for three summers there a while back. I would race at Selingrove and tracks like that, and I'd go from one race to another in a trailer I had. Mostly I would stay up near Beavertown, which was in the Pennsylvania mountains. I always had to be near mountains.

There were some weekends when I'd be traveling two thousand miles getting to one race and then another. I was making good money, more than sixty thousand dollars, but I was also running an awful lot of races, one hundred maybe in a year. And I was winning maybe fifty. That's an awful lot of races to win that much money. But I liked it. I liked being able to tell some promoters I wouldn't take their deal unless they gave me *x* dollars or whatever. I figured running all those races was a small price to pay for having my freedom from the regular racing bodies.

I was in my thirties already when I was doing all this, and maybe if I had been younger I would have looked into USAC racing before I did. I mean, I might have cut my hair and gone through all that smiling and saying "howdydo" to everybody, and acting like those other guys around the tracks. But I wasn't young anymore, and the way I figured was that my life was pretty good without all that stuff.

But it started to get to me that with all the races I was winning, people still didn't recognize me for what I was doing in racing. I was winning probably more races than anybody, but nobody knew about it. Also, I wasn't too happy with being called World Dirt Track Champion and Dirt Track King, like a lot of people were advertising and promoting me.

I had done some racing on asphalt, and done O.K., and I thought being called somethin' like Dirt Track King meant I didn't want to race on something else, or couldn't. But I really was lookin' to get into some asphalt racing.

I started doing some running in USAC sprints at the beginning of '74. I think a lot of people wanted to keep me out, not let me have a license, but my record for so many years forced them, I think, to let me run with them.

So, anyway, I'm at this race, this sprint race in Cincinnati, and I'm getting to meet a lot of the guys and gettin' friendly, you know. Sammy Sessions was maybe the nicest of 'em all. He acted like he wanted to really help. He and a couple of other guys said, "Why don't you come down to Indy in May and we'll introduce you around, and maybe you'll get yourself a ride?"

Well, I hadn't really thought about Indy or even championship racing at all. But I knew that in USAC the only way to make any money is in championship racing. So I said, "Swell, I'll take you up on it."

So I went to Indy on May sixth, the day the Speedway opened for drivers, and couldn't believe the way the place looked. I mean, it was much bigger than I even expected. I was used to driving half-mile and mile tracks, and the Speedway is two and a half miles around. It just comes at you and hits you right in the eye.

But the funny thing is, when some of the drivers came out on the track in their cars, I didn't think much of 'em. I mean, here's A. J. Foyt or somebody, and he's goin' around, and it looks like he's strokin' it. Not hustling. But man, was I wrong about that! I didn't realize until I was there for a while that these guys were so good it just *looked* like they were strokin' it. But these guys were going

Jan Opperman

41

195, 200 miles an hour and just makin' it look easy. I think
that's what surprised me the most, the way these guys
made it all look so easy. I realize now that the guys who
drive the USAC championship cars are probably the best
drivers you're ever gonna find. Until I was up close to that
scene, I didn't realize how good these guys are.

One of the guys I met up with my first time at Indy was
Parnelli Jones. He ran the racing team which had Al
Unser and Mario Andretti running for it. And it turned
out he was looking for a third driver for the '74 race. He
told me he was pretty impressed with the fact that I had
been running ninety-five, one hundred races a year. "I
used to run sixty races a year," he told me, "and I thought
that was pretty tough. So I know you can drive one of
these things."

But, before he let me take one of his cars on the track,
he made me go take a haircut. This was a chance I couldn't
afford to pass up, so I went and cut three inches off my
own hair. But when I got back and showed Parnelli, it still
wasn't cut short enough for him. I mean, Parnelli wears a
toupée trimmed real nice, and he wanted me to go back
and get some more of my hair cut off. So I did it.

And Parnelli gave me his third car, which had to be a
pretty good deal for a guy's first year at the Speedway, and
I went out and qualified it for the thirty-second spot, which
just barely got me into the race. But I was in, and I finished
twenty-first. Actually, I was running tenth and goin' good
when I spun out on the eighty-fifth lap. Something just
shook loose on the car; I don't really know what happened.

But I was pretty satisfied with that finish my first shot at
the Speedway. I thought things would get better for me,
but really, they haven't. I've been doing good in USAC
sprints ever since I started with them in '74. I've won a
lot of features and finished high in the national point
standings. But Indy hasn't been a good trip for me yet.

In '75 I had a lot of problems with the car I was supposed to drive, and I never did qualify it. In '76 I got the
last qualifying spot, and got it home sixteenth and was
still running when they stopped the race because of the

rain. I was running for the Longhorn Racing Team out of Texas.

I used to say I wouldn't get into thinking about these kinds of big races and the big tracks. But racing means more to me probably than I ever even realized a few years ago. I'm never gonna go entirely "establishment." I won't show up at your party with a suit and tie on. No way. But I want to keep goin' in racing and then sock enough money away into my home and for my wife and kids, and then get out of it.

I'm thinking it's gonna take me a while to get all of my strength back for racing because of the accident I had in the Hoosier Hundred in '76. I was in the hospital about five weeks, you know, and when you're laid up that long, you get real weak. I had a cerebral concussion, and it affected my left side for a while. I felt off-balance and weak, and I got tired real quick. It was bad during the time of the year when I was trying to get firewood and stuff into the house. Winter in the mountains can be very hard, so I was trying to get everything we needed put aside for us. But I couldn't work like I wanted to because I was still feeling weak. I had some problems talkin' too. I was doing some mumbling there for a while, a little hard to understand.

But gradually, everything's been coming back, and I don't see no problems as far as goin' back racing. The guys I've been with, the crews and all, they all expect me back doin' my thing as usual.

From where we are in Noxon, a town of only about one thousand people, it's hard to go racing because I'm so far from connections. Sometimes, to get to a race I'll have to catch a plane in Spokane, a hundred thirty-five miles west of where I start out from, or I can go to Missoula, catch something going to Denver, and then go on from there. But, hey, nobody forces me to live way up here. It's what's right for me and the family.

My wife's Mary. We've been married eleven years. She and I've had three kids—Krystal, who was born in 1968; another girl, Jay Lou, born in '71, and then when we finally had a boy in '73, we named him Brother Boy. I like to call all males brother and all females sister. Altogether we've got three daughters because my girl, Teacia, from my first wife, is also with us. She was born in '62. I got married when I was twenty-one and stayed with that wife for five years. It wasn't one of the best things I ever did, marrying at that age and marrying that particular girl. I wasn't mature enough to handle it, and the whole thing was kind of bad. I had lots of things to get out of my system during those years—including the dope smokin' and other women and all o' that.

Sometimes people ask me, they wonder how my kids like living up here, way out in nowhere. Well, they all sure seem to like it. It's a good way to live, and we try to keep it good. We've got a little cattle we're raising here, some cows and things, chickens and stuff.

It's been said in the papers that I've got some sort of home or something for wayward kids up here. Well, the truth is, I've had some kids come up and spend some time with us in one of the cabins we've been puttin' up. We'll put up anybody who needs a little help. I'd really like to make something up here to help kids. I feel if you can get a kid who needs help up here in this environment, he's just gotta get straightened out. Not just kids. People in general—all ages, men, women, everybody.

But I don't want anybody thinkin' I've got a high-falutin' production up here for helpin' kids. I'd really like to sometime, but nothing like that's going on now.

I'm thinking something like this is gonna happen when I'm done racin'. I'll start preaching maybe full time. When I'm off racing, I usually can't give any sermons on Sundays or anything, so we've had regular Tuesday night prayer meetings. Some of the folks wish I would forget about the racing and stay and preach on Sundays. But I can't do that yet. When I've got enough stashed away, then I can get out of racing and work for Christianity all the way. Right now I've got another minister up here who does some preaching and sermons.

Before I discovered Jesus, I was a typical race driver,

you know, on an ego trip. And I used to party. There wasn't one race when I didn't have some woman or another with me. I mean, I dig chicks. I still like to look at 'em, but I'm straight now with my old lady. Mary, my wife, that is.

Like I say, Christianity is where it's at for me. I've learned to praise the Lord for everything. If I went out *Jan* tomorrow and tore off both my arms in a race car, I'd still *Opperman* get out of the car and praise the Lord.

45

bill simpson

BILL SIMPSON first came to Indy to sell
auto-racing suits but returned a few years later
to compete. Simpson is a maverick figure
in the sport, a man who racing people
did not take to at first.

I was a hot rodder in high school. This was in the South Bay area, Los Angeles. Back then LA wasn't criss-crossed with freeways. You could go down to where the Harbor Freeway is now. And it was, like, three lanes. And you wouldn't see a car on that street but once every two hours.

Back then it was called Figueroa. What is now the Harbor Freeway was then known as Figueroa Street. A three-laner, practically deserted. Perfect for street racing. There's still a Figueroa, but it's not where it used to be.

The racing crowd would meet in a hamburger place. All the hot-dog drivers hung out there. And around nine o'clock everybody would start trucking on down to Figueroa—sometimes three hundred to four hundred guys—to stage drag races.

It was a real scene. Some strange guys. You're really asking me to go back a long way, but like, I can remember one guy who lived in a wooden house on Western Avenue in LA. He would sleep in his garage, and his living room was, like, where he worked on his racer. More room there, see?

Anyway, he built the car in his house, in his living room. The kitchen was the motor room. And he had to stay out in the garage. Because it was only a one-bedroom place. And he knocked the wall out of the bedroom. It was a really old house.

There was another guy. Called him Big Willie. He's still around. A black guy. He'd drag-race his motorcycle. He lived on the second floor of an old house, and he'd ride his motorcycle up the stairs and into his bedroom, and he'd lay down in bed and putter around with his motorcycle.

I had a '49 Chevrolet. A friend of mine who had a muffler shop was one of the first guys that messed around with a supercharger. Put a GMC supercharger on a 331 Chrysler. And stuck it in my '49 Chevy that I used to drive on the street. And we'd terrorize all the street racers.

Hundreds of guys down to Figueroa. And Wednesday and Friday nights is when this would take place. It'd be around midnight when things would get started. And we'd race all night or until the cops came. I can remember being out there sometimes when the sun came up.

The cops would come now and then. It'd look like a bomb exploded in the middle of the crowd. Everybody would split. Usually, the cops would swoop in with quite a few cruisers and try to block all the side streets around Figueroa. And those guys that didn't get away got arrested. For staging speed contests. Or drunk and disorderly. I got nailed a couple of times.

No big deal. I was on my own as a kid. When I was twelve, I didn't live with my parents any longer. My father got real sick. And my mother became an alcoholic. It was beyond me. So I just left. I went to live with an aunt, who was nearby.

She didn't care what I did. I went to school, had a part-time job, and fiddled with my car. And that's all I did. School at that time was four hours of class, and four hours of a job. The four hours on the job were credited—like high school work. They used to have a program like that in California. No more.

The job I got credit for was in an upholstery shop. I made two dollars an hour, a dollar seventy-five, something like that. I delivered furniture, swept up the shop, made buttons, fixed sewing machines.

I graduated high school in 1957. And I decided to get a full-time job related to cars. I went to a friend of mine who had a muffler shop. This muffler shop, though, specialized in hopping up cars. That was what I did for about a year and a half. At the same time the shop sponsored an all-out drag-racing car that I built and drove.

At that time I wasn't thinking of doing it for a living.

Hell, I was just a kid. I didn't have any idea what I wanted to do or where I'd be next week. I started making money with the car. I was good at it. At that time there were probably twelve guys in the country that were running drag racers 180 miles an hour or better. All California boys. And I was one of them. Fact is, when they had drag races in the East, they had to fly us California boys there to race. Made a lot of money at it. And was going great until I come back to the Coast and went out to the San Fernando Dragway and had a really big wreck. You know, a double-throwdown crash. And we didn't have any safety equipment then. And I got some hospital-sheet time out of it.

And I lay there in the hospital trying to figure out how the hell I was going to stop that from happening to me the next time. See, the problem back then was that guys couldn't always stop the cars. Same thing happened to me. The brake handle broke off in my hand. And there was nothing I could do. I took my foot back off the clutch and let the motor come down, but I just went right off the drag strip, hit a pole and some rocks, and ended up with a lot of broken bones. And a pipe landed on my arm and gave me a superbad burn.

So I thought: I've got to figure out a way to stop that from happening because when I come out of the hospital, I'm gonna go drag-racing again. Which I did. I came out of the hospital and built a new car. And I went to a friend of mine who had a surplus business, and he gave me a parachute that they stop jet airplanes with. And I held it in my lap and made a pass and threw the parachute out, and it worked really good. And that was sort of the beginning of a business and was directly related to racing. 'Cause all my pals, all the guys that were hot dogs at the time, heard about it and called me and said, "Hey, make one for me." And so I made them and I was selling them, you know, for forty or fifty dollars. And a business developed.

What I did was, I rented a four-car garage. Half the

garage was set up for my race car, and the other half was for making parachutes. Pretty soon the business thing got booming beyond my expectations. I had to quit racing one year to keep up with the business.

In a short time I was out of the garage. I went down to Vermont Avenue and bought a piece of property. Paid six thousand dollars. An old vacant lot. And I put an ad in *Drag News*. The ad said if anybody was a drag racer or in the construction business, or if he was a carpenter, plumber, whatever, to call me. I got all kinds of telephone calls, and what I did is, I rounded up a crew of guys that were all drag racers, and we put up a building. All of us hammering and nailing and pouring cement.

I paid them. It cost me ten thousand dollars. I built a four-thousand-square-foot building. After I moved into my new place, I found a really good secretary and a kid who soon knew as much about what I was doing as I did. At that point I started falling back into racing.

The racing for me was just for fun. I was making my money on Simpson Drag Chute Company. That's what it was called then. I raced cars. One year I raced boats. Then all of a sudden some rear-engine cars appeared at Indianapolis. Jim Clark one year blew everybody's doors in. [Clark won the Indy 500 in 1965 at a speed of 150.686 miles per hour.]

When they made these cars available to club racers, the rear-engine cars, I got one of the first Lotuses, a rear-engine Lotus. And I started cleaning house. I won lots of races. And I really dug it.

I kept an eye on business. Came up with new ideas. Like the fire suits for drivers. At the time drivers were wearing these chicken-shit driver's suits that gave hardly any protection against fire. I wrote a letter to fabric companies and chemical companies. And DuPont replied that they had an experimental fabric called Nomex, and they'd send it to us to try out. We made the first Nomex driving suit.

And, hell, all of a sudden business tripled. 'Cause

everybody wanted one of those things. It stopped being just chutes we made. And it started being more profitable than ever. [Simpson Safety Equipment, which specializes in auto-race gear, grosses more than $1.5 million a year.]

The first time I went to Indianapolis was in 1967. I had absolutely no idea I would ever go there as a race driver. In '67 I was there to show the Nomex suits. I did a little demonstration for USAC people to show how much better Nomex was than the cotton suits being used. I did the same thing for Goodyear and Firestone tire companies, which were investing heavily in the sport then. I remember Goodyear ordered fire suits for all their drivers in the 500 that year. There were seventeen drivers.

And that year I met Foyt and Gurney and Gordon Johncock. I met all those cats that I'd heard about all my life. And I was superimpressed. It was a big thrill to me. I met those people, and I got to be friends with them. And I'd tell them, "Yeah. I got a Formula-B car back in California." And they'd say, "Aw, that's okay, kid. You just keep after it."

And I came back to California, and I was just genuinely pumped. I decided to make an effort to really excel in a rear-engine car, which I did. Like, I ran in 1968 something like twenty-eight races. And I either sat on the pole or in the front row at every race qualifying. I would either win the race, or my car would break, and that was kind of my record.

USAC at that time had just gone into running some road races. In December '68 I went up to Riverside [California] and I watched the Rex Mays 300. And I decided I could be competitive. So when the next Rex Mays 300 came around, I asked in. And I remember I got a really bad reception by a couple of USAC officials who told me they didn't like sports-car guys and they didn't think I had any business being there. If I made any mistakes, I'd be out fast. They gave me a conditional license to run. I ran that first race, the 300, and finished sixth. Which I thought was not too bad.

I didn't say a word after. I just packed my car up and

split and I got paid twenty-eight hundred dollars. And I began racing oval tracks too.

The business by now had moved. A new place. The other place was four thousand square foot on an eight-thousand-square-foot lot. We are operating now with fifteen thousand five hundred square foot of manufacturing space. And we just broke ground for forty-one thousand more square foot. This is in Torrance, California.

Meantime I was working my way up on the Indy car circuit. In 1970, when I came to Indy, I came with a car I owned. I came to Indy to compete.

At that time, 1970, long hair was a subject of controversy. I had long hair and a Teddy Roosevelt mustache. To the veteran drivers it was, I guess, an unsettling sight. I also had a bit of an attitude. By that time I was putting away a lot of money. I was socking a hundred thousand dollars a year into my bank account. Which made me kind of arrogant.

I think I've changed. But as I say, back then I had a chip on my shoulder. I had it wherever I went. It got me into scenes, you know. Like, one night at some joint, a fellow took my barstool when I went to the bathroom. And when I came back, I said, "Hey, man. You're sitting on my seat." And he said, "Well, you know, you ain't here, and I am." So I said, "Get off my seat." And when he said I wasn't big enough to move him off the seat, I knocked him over the bar.

Why I was that way I'm not so sure. I didn't have a boyhood that was very happy, which probably had an effect. Anyway, when I got to Indy as a driver, the veterans didn't take to me. Like, 1970 they were going to cut my hair off and they were going to do this and they were going to do that. And they didn't want me around there because I didn't fit in with their program. And Foyt, Al and Bobby Unser, and Lloyd Ruby—they come around and were going to cut my hair. And I said, "You ain't cutting my fucking hair." And my mechanics all were long hairs from

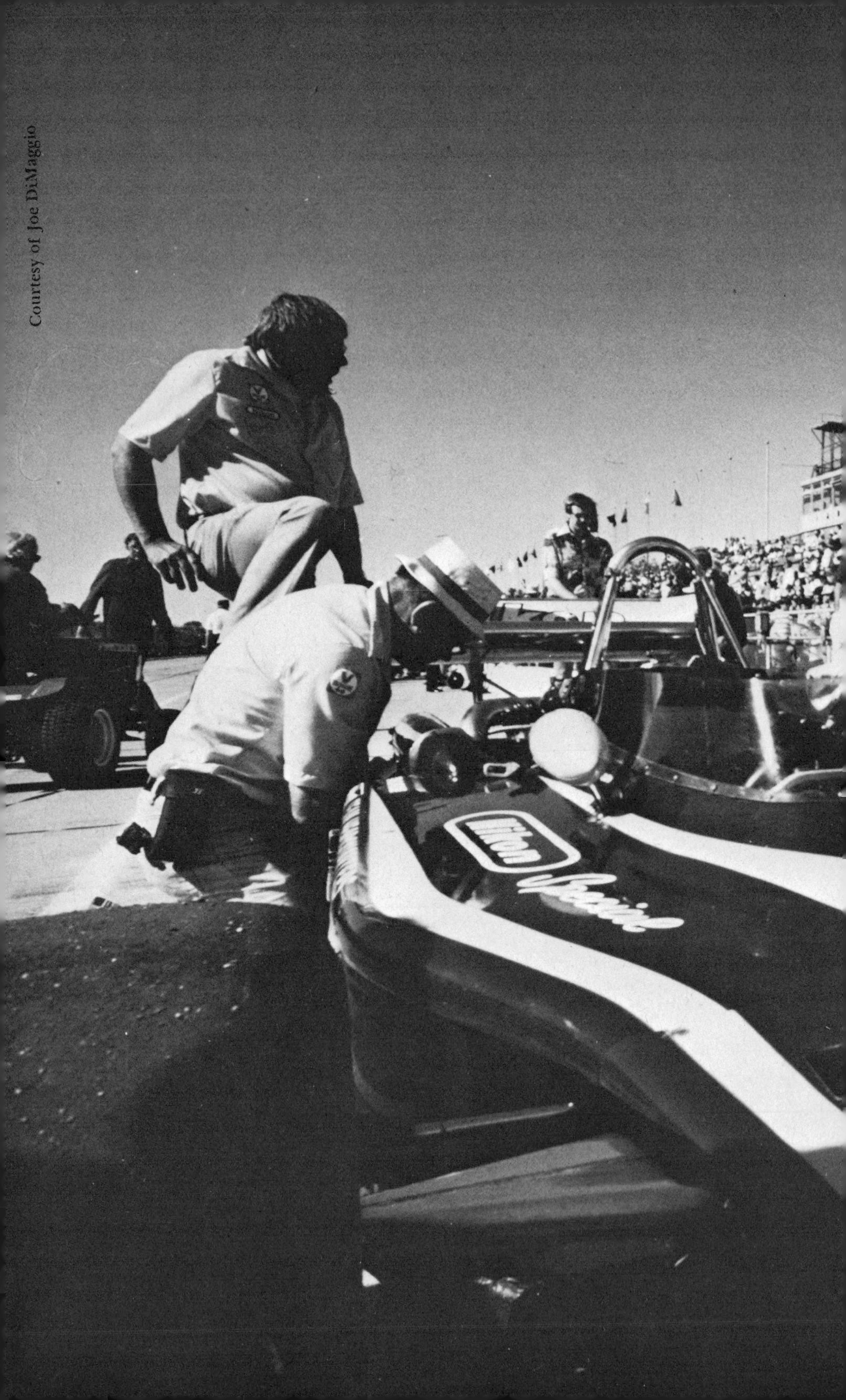

Courtesy of Joe DiMaggio

southern California, and they all got up and said, "No, there ain't going to be no fucking haircutting in here, or there's going to be a hell of a fistfight." So they turned around and left.

That was the start of a very bad period for me with USAC officials and drivers. They gave me a very hard time. And, looking back, I guess I gave them a hard time. I brought a lot of it on with my attitude.

I went to a USAC race in Argentina. Nineteen seventy-one. I was ordered to go to a luncheon. And I told Dick King—it was his first official job in USAC as the competition director for the championship division—I told Dick King: "You can get bent. I have my race car here, and when I'm at the race track, you can tell me what to do. But when I ain't by my race car, you aren't telling me a thing. Now you hit the road."

He got all upset and real tight-jawed about it. But anyway I had another place to go. I went to a luncheon with some legal students, and I met a woman I eventually married. Her name's Cristina, and she's an Argentine lawyer.

Most of the time I was in Argentina—two and a half weeks—when I wasn't racing, I was with Cristina. The funny thing is that when I was with her at night, her aunt was too. It was the Argentine custom to be chaperoned. The aunt stuck on her like flypaper while I was around. But I thought it was a gas.

Anyway my run-in with Dick King was just one of the problems I had with USAC. And when I got back to the States and turned up for the next race at Phoenix, I was told I'd been fined one thousand dollars. I went in and talked to Dick King. Dick King says, "Until you pay that one-thousand-dollar fine, you're not getting credentials to come in." So I wrote him a check and paid the fine.

For a few years my luck was bad at Indy. I passed my driver's test in 1970. But I couldn't qualify. The usual reasons. Blown engines and what not. In 1971 I thought I was going to qualify. I zipped along real good for three laps, and in the final turn of lap number four the engine let go. It dropped my speed just enough to get bumped the next weekend of qualifying. In '72 I ate all my pieces. The car kept blowing parts.

I made a decision. I decided I couldn't afford to race anymore. It was costing me too much money. I'd spent a couple of hundred thousand dollars on my own car and was going no place. I figured, though, that I now had enough experience to get a ride from someone else. If I couldn't get a ride, I wasn't going to race.

To make sure I wasn't tempted to go back on the decision, I sold all my race stuff. All my Indianapolis gear was sold, and I disbanded my operation completely. Sold my truck and my transporter. Sold my tools. Sold everything.

The next year [1973] I hooked up with Rolla Vollstedt. I agreed to drive for him. It was a bad year. I was at the Speedway for a month, and I crashed that car of Vollstedt's really bad. Other things happened. You know, Jim Malloy was a pal of mine, and he was killed the year before that. Art Pollard was killed the day after I crashed. And Swede Savage was killed during the race.

Up to that point I'd always felt there was no way I could ever be hurt in one of those cars. I lost it coming off a turn. I was running, like, 189 miles an hour. I lost it and went backward into the inside wall. And it scared the hell out of me. I didn't really want to get back into one of them cars.

They fixed the car. And I went back out and tried to qualify on the last day of qualifying. And the car wasn't right. And it was wiggling. And it scared the shit out of me. Like it set me back ten years. I went to Pocono, and the car was doing the same thing, and I quit. I told Vollstedt that I was not mentally up to doing a good job. I quit and came home.

I sat around until about September. Then Joe Hunt called me. I'd known Joe since I was fourteen years old, since I first got into races. Joe made my magnetos for me when I was a kid. Joe called me on the phone and said, "What are you doing?" I said, "I'm not doing anything."

He says, "Would you be interested in driving my car at Ontario?" I said, "I don't know. Let me think about it."

See, I didn't know for sure whether I wanted to sit back in one of those cars again. Finally, though, I called Joe back and said, "Yeah, I'll drive your car at Ontario."

Now, I know I'm not in the caliber of Mario Andretti or Bobby Unser or A. J. Foyt. I do feel, though, I'm as good as the average USAC driver. But Vollstedt's car made me wonder. Then I got into Joe Hunt's car. Ran ten laps at 188 miles an hour. And I'm thinking to myself all this time: Man . . . it's not me. It was that car I was riding in. Now I had a car that would respond, and I could feel what it was doing. I came back in, and I told Joe: "I want to thank you, man. Because all of a sudden I got my confidence back."

And he said, "Well, go out there and run some." So I went out, and I ended up running his car 192 miles an hour. Come time to qualify, and we pitched the motor. Flat blew it right out of the car. And that was the first year that they had the two-lap qualifying in the hundred-mile heat races the next day. That killed us. We didn't get the car down until the next day at noon. So we had absolutely no chance to make a qualification attempt. We put the car in line with the new engine in it—with no practice. And we went out, and they dropped the green flag, and the car wouldn't shift. They'd screwed up when they put the shift linkage on it.

So Joe apologized. He gave me all the money that he'd made, which was eleven hundred and some dollars for my part of the thing. [Simpson finished seventeenth at Ontario in 1973.] Which I thought was pretty nice of him. And he asked me if I would be willing to drive the car at Texas.

I said, "Sure, I'll take your car to Texas." Which I did. I drove his car. I pulled it down to Texas 'cause he didn't have a pit crew, and I qualified the car down there twelfth. It ended up, though, breaking down on the parade lap. So I told Joe, I said, "Man, I don't need anymore of this. I'm going to pass."

Bill
Simpson

58

Indy came around again [1974], and I was determined this time to make the race. Two, three years I'd had nothing but disappointment. I went back there and my practice speeds were 184, 185, 186 miles an hour every day. But I tried to outsmart myself.

The car was sticking awfully good in the front. That is, when it cornered, it was holding its ground. Just a teeny bit of looseness in it. I couldn't leave well enough alone. So I told the mechanic, "What I'd like to do is drop the front wing a sixteenth of an inch." So he dropped the front wing a sixteenth of an inch.

Bill Simpson

59

Now I went out to qualify, and that mother was pushing so bad that I could not drive it through the corner. I drove down into turn one, I went past the gate with my foot on the gas and then would have to back off and just let the car coast, and pick the throttle up again. I whitewalled the right front tire—it touched the wall.

And I qualified at 181.6 or something like that. I came in and everybody was pissed at me. I said, "Man, I did the best I could." But I was thinking: Man, here we go again. I'm going to get bumped. Then other guys started going out. And it turned out I was right smack dab in the middle of the field. I'd made the race.

All those years, though, there was another thing going on. A kind of running battle with USAC and other drivers. And, I guess, with Bill Simpson as well.

Continuous hassles. I was always being fined. Always into it with somebody. It almost came to a fistfight one day with Gary Bettenhausen over something that happened during a race. And I got out of the car. And he came running over like he does. And I told him, "Go ahead. Hit me if you want. I'll break your back." It didn't come to blows, though.

My personal life sometimes got messy too. Like one time in 1971—in fact, it was the day after New Year's—there were three of us in my office. And we got in a hassle, and we destroyed the office, knocked all the windows out. Holes in the wall.

I had a case on the wall with big iron rods that held it up. And one of the guys got hold of a rod and was going to use it on the other guy. I grabbed him and smacked him in the eye. He wouldn't let go of the rod, though. He wanted to hit the other guy.

Bill Simpson

60

So I screamed, "Hit the wall with it, hit the wall!" And that's what he did. About a week after, a girl I knew came by to visit. I was all black and blue. Cuts on my face. She saw what had happened. And offered to paint a mural over the wall.

And that's what you saw in the office. The mural she painted. And what it was, was a montage of images that are supposed to represent how she saw me. We locked up the office on a Friday, and she painted all weekend.

At the center of the mural was a race car with a woman sitting on the nose of the car. And behind that you have me fighting. And way back is a little biplane because I'm really into antique airplanes, I love them. And a boat because that's an interest of mine, too. And the airplane on the extreme left represents my travels. I do a lot of traveling. And what looks like bullets are disembodied penises. I don't really understand that. I don't understand the trees. And I don't understand the birds or the stars.

The fact that the woman has no head—just a body—well, it's definitely not a romantic view of a woman, and I think it's probably because my relations with women have been many and short-lived.

When I saw it, I told her I didn't like it. I said that I just didn't dig it. And she said, "Billy, that's the way I see you. And I'm me. And you're you. And I painted what I saw." And I said, "Well, if that's what you think, then that's what it's gonna stay." What it says about me is true. And that's a fact you can't change.

Just the same, it was about that time I made an effort to change my attitude, particularly in the racing scene, so that I would become more well liked. A concerted effort to be more diplomatic and to try to get along with people.

You find that you get a hell of a lot more by being person-able with somebody than by being a jerk. It doesn't matter who you are or what you have.

My personality made a hundred-and-eighty-degree change. I saw a lot of things in myself that I didn't like. It was a time that I had to get along with other people, and I had never in my whole life been in a position where I had to do that. And I'm not unhappy over the things I went through. I can look back at myself—the early part of 1971—and say, "Man, that guy was really an ass."

And since those early hassles with guys like Gary Bettenhausen and the veterans like Foyt and Unser and Lloyd Ruby, I've become friendly with them. Lloyd Ruby and Bobby Unser both have endorsed my company's equipment. And Al Unser is always saying, "Boy, you sure have cleaned up your act, Simpson. We just can't get over it." Like I get that kind of comment all the time.

The kicker to the story is this: Christmastime 1973 I received an airmail special delivery. It was from USAC, and it arrived on Christmas Eve, about two in the afternoon. A Christmas present in the form of a check.

A check for twenty-two hundred dollars. It was signed by Dick King, the man I'd given a hard time in Argentina. A note with it said, "Thanks for your cooperation. I'm sure you'll find this helpful." The money represented half of the fines that I'd paid in my first two years with USAC. A good Christmas present.

john martin

JOHN MARTIN's racing operation is special.
In a sport in which most drivers are financed
by big corporations Martin is not. He puts his
own money on the line . . . and somehow makes out.

I'm a farmboy. I was brought up on a farm in Missouri. I didn't even know what Indy was. I was too busy walking behind a team of horses and a plow.

My father was gone quite a bit. He was a carpenter and bricklayer and shipyard worker and so forth. When I was a boy, he worked in different towns all over the country.

From the age of nine, I ran the farm. I plowed forty acres, planted it, harvested. My older brother was sixteen then and on his own. He was away from home. I was in charge.

I'd get up just a little after daylight. Me and my mom would milk the cows. Had fourteen cows. In the wintertime you had to cut the ice for the cows so they could drink. I'd milk them and get the milk in cream cans, then change my clothes and head for the schoolhouse.

It was a one-room schoolhouse with a big potbellied stove in one end of the room. And on dark days we'd light up gas lanterns. That was all we used for light. Grade school was in that one room. I started my first year on one side of the room and graduated eight years later on the other side of the room. One teacher for all the grades. About thirty kids altogether.

Some kids had to walk two and a half, three miles to school. I was lucky. I was close to school. After school I'd hurry home. I'd try to have the chores done before dark because we didn't have electricity either in the barn or in our house. Just kerosene lamps. So to keep from working after dark you'd hustle.

There wasn't much time for anything but farm work. After school I might listen to fifteen minutes of "Sky King" on the battery-powered radio. Then I'd go to work. After dinner, if the day's work was done, then I could listen to more radio programs. I remember "Amos 'n Andy" and "Dragnet." A lot of time the batteries would get so weak, you'd have to practically stick your head inside the radio to hear.

Usually after the supper dishes were done, before we went to bed, my mother and sister would sit and sing and play the piano. That was our entertainment at home.

Sometimes, though, after dark, I'd go horseback riding or hunting. After you'd do your chores and eat supper, why you'd go possum hunting or coon hunting. Go up through the woods. It's light enough to see, and you just follow the bay of the dogs. And if it gets a little cool, you stop and build a fire and tell stories until the dog trees a coon or something. And then you go after him.

A lot of times you'd go out and it'd get cloudy. You had to know your way around the woods. And long as you knew the lay of the land, you were okay. Long as you knew which way the river ran, or that moss grew on the north side of trees, you never were lost. You might not know exactly where you were, but you weren't lost. You knew how to get home.

Horseback riding was a big interest of mine. I worked a year and a half for my first saddle horse. I cleared fifteen acres of new ground for other people. I belonged to a saddle club. It was in town, which was, like, seven miles away. A little town of about twenty-five hundred, called Licking. Where we lived was out in the boondocks.

When my father was home, he made donuts. I always hated that because that was an added chore that I had to do. I had to really rush home and clean up the room he used for making the donuts. He made about three hundred dozen there in the farmhouse with propane gas and gasoline lanterns. He had a route he'd haul the donuts after they were made. He'd start making them about midnight. And he'd make close to a hundred dozen an hour. Him and my mom.

He made donuts when he ran out of jobs, or things got really rough. But he had what they call flour asthma. He was allergic to wheat flour. And it affected his health. So he could only hack it for like six months at a time. A heck of a thing for a donut maker to have.

As I got older, I got into saddle horses. I was going to be a rodeo buster, bronc buster. A lot of time we'd sneak onto what they called the Lost Valley Ranch that was down on Current River. We'd go down and we'd play rodeo. We'd ride Missouri mules. They were wild. We'd corner them up and rope them and tie them down. And then crawl on them 'til they threw you off.

The mules belonged to the man who owned Lost Valley. But they were never worked. They were just raised and were never touched by human beings. But they were the hardest bucking animal that ever was created—a Missouri mule.

We got good at riding them. We did calf roping and we'd ride the bulls. The owner of the place didn't find out for several years. By that time I was about to discover the automobile.

We left the farm when I was in junior high school. I started playing a lot of football for Houston [Missouri] High School. We won the southern division championship. That's where I graduated from in 1957. Houston, Missouri, was the county seat for Texas County, Missouri.

At that time, my father ran a filling station. Martin's DX Filling Station. My father was Charles Martin. He had an arrangement with me. He credited me for all the labor that I did. Like two, three o'clock in the morning, the big trucks go by, and I'd get up and go out and do the repair work. Whatever money there was for labor, I kept that. He kept whatever money he made off the tires or the tubes. That was the arrangement. And for that kind of money I didn't mind getting up at three in the morning. I got to really know cars too. I overhauled my first engine my junior year in high school.

We were open all night on Friday nights because that was the big weekend, where people came down to the dams and the lakes to go fishing. It was tough during football season. 'Cause we played our games on Friday nights. I'd get home about midnight. Then I'd keep the station open from midnight 'til eight o'clock the next morning because that was when people came from the city to the country. And then Sunday nights—lotta times I'd work Sunday afternoons while my father would sleep. He'd keep it open all Sunday night. So it was open twenty-four hours Sunday.

Like I say, I was just a country boy. A big time for me was to go to Saint Louis. A real good buddy of mine would get his father's '39 Chevy. We'd pool five dollars each and drive to Saint Louis for a wild Saturday night. And all that consisted of was just driving around, looking at the town, and then going back home on Sunday.

Saint Louis was like two hundred and fifty miles away. And we just drove around and tried to find the addresses of all the friends we had from home who were living now in Saint Louis. We didn't see them half the time; we'd just drive by.

That was when I was seventeen, eighteen years old. The wildest thing down home was like a square dance on Saturday night. See, everybody went to town on Saturday night. That was the big night. And like the rowdy goings-on were on one end of the town. There was a place what you called Owl's Tavern. It was more like a saloon. All the guys would come in the town once a week and kick up their heels, get smashed, fight, and wind up in jail.

But Saint Louis seemed to me at that time the biggest city in the world. It was amazing how many people and houses could be all in one place. You had the country. And the rest of the world was Saint Louis.

After I graduated from high school, I was in the merchant marines. Sailed out of Chicago. And then I came back and went to work in Saint Louis. That's where all the country boys went. And a lot of them worked for General Motors and McDonnell-Douglas. I worked for an independent repair shop as a mechanic.

While I was in Saint Louis, the Pontiacs were really running down at Daytona Beach. And I started getting the race feeling. I'd read about it and see pictures and TV shots of it. This was back when Fireball Roberts was running. And at the time I was working on Pontiacs.

So I started taking scrap engine parts that were junk and putting them together and built me a little B-gas drag racer out of a '34 Ford. And we called it *Country Boy,* naturally. It had a picture of a country boy with a wheat straw and a double-barreled shotgun on the back of it. And with *Country Boy* I was ready to go racing.

Country Boy was unusual in this respect: It had a start off of the line that was just unreal. But it would fade out on the other end bad.

There were other cars that were faster. But the start I got with *Country Boy* would make them lose their cool. Ninety percent of the time they'd blow it. They'd miss a shift or break an axle. There was just no way they could beat me off the line.

That wasn't all either. I had a friend of mine who would talk *Country Boy* up. He'd needle the other drivers and mechanics. Kind of trying to psych them up. And I believed it worked. It made them overanxious. And in that state they'd make mistakes.

We had fifty-two wins that year in NHRA competitions. The competition was for trophies and five dollars. Yeah. Five dollars. They'd pay you off down at the barrel at the end of the drag strip. The drag strip was right across the river in Alton, Illinois.

Racing then was mostly for fun. For profit I continued to be a Pontiac engine builder. I was an engine specialist for three years at Tom's Pontiac. I met a guy that was racing what we call sporty cars. And he had a homemade monster with a Pontiac engine in it.

I got involved in going to the races with him. I saw some things he was doing wrong with the engines. He had the compression rate so high it just knocked the pistons right out of it. So I got involved with building his engines for him. And it got me to thinking that it might be fun to try racing sporty cars for a while.

This was in 1963. I purchased me a nice shiny black Sting Ray. I went to driver's school in Enid, Oklahoma. It was my first attempt to drive a race car, really. And at Enid, I won first overall everything at the school.

I won several races that year. At that point it was just like a hobby. People said I had a lot of natural driving ability. But I didn't think much about it. At that particular time I had a really good position at the dealership—tune-up and engine specialist. It was fantastic money for a country boy. Twelve thousand dollars a year. I was content. I didn't owe anybody anything. I could go where I wanted to go. To me it was a beautiful life.

Then, in 1964, I decided, as they say, to stand on the gas. To get serious. I wanted to see if I was good or not. I became the A-Production champion in SCCA's Midwest Division in '65.

Believe me I worked like crazy to be good. It was me and a friend of mine who was a mechanical engineer. He had a couple of master's degrees. And we were living in a place out in the country, on the outskirts of Saint Louis. A bunch of us renting a place.

And what we did, we had the whole thing programmed very tightly. Each of us worked eight hours a day at our jobs. He was an aircraft engineer. He worked in the solar simulator for McDonnell-Douglas. And he'd use the computers there to figure out things about our cars.

Our garage had a gravel floor. And we'd mock up the car on a beer keg. And go from there. We'd work all day Friday and come home, load up our cars that we'd been working on all week, and we'd get ready for the race.

We wouldn't run any race we couldn't get to within twelve hours. We had a twelve-hour circle around Saint Louis. Say we were racing in Milwaukee. We'd drive all night Friday night and sleep a couple hours before registration on Saturday morning. Then we'd unload the race cars, get through inspections, qualify the cars. That night we'd have an honest night's sleep. We had a curfew to be in bed by nine o'clock on Saturday night. We let the parties alone. Had to.

Sunday there was a qualifying race and then the main race. After, we'd load the cars up and drive back to Saint Louis just in time to take a shower, change clothes, and go to work.

It went like that for two years. During the week—that was when it really got hectic. We arrived at the figure 3.6 hours of sleep as the amount of sleep we needed to be alert and productive. Anything less, we just couldn't hack it. We'd just really run out of gas.

To keep those long hours, we ate a lot. More than the average person. Just like a race car. The more output you get, the more input you gotta have. We'd eat exactly at seven and then again at midnight. Steak and potatoes. Usually steak and potatoes. One of the guys would do the cooking and the other would do the dishes. That was it, though, for both meals. Steak and potatoes. And maybe some spinach.

Anyway, the work paid off. Won thirteen out of fourteen starts. And so I decided to turn professional. That's when Indianapolis started sounding good.

In 1966 I raced USAC stock cars. That year I moved to Milwaukee in order to build a race car with another guy who talked me into moving. I left my job and everything. All my security. I found a job, though, with a dealership in Milwaukee. I'd work eight hours there, and then eight hours on the stock car.

In '67 the car got bought by a Plymouth dealer in Kenosha, Wisconsin. And at that time Gordon Johncock was driving for him. So Johncock and myself were the team's drivers. I took care of both cars. It was a rough time. The reason it got rough was the dealer went bankrupt on me with like seventeen weeks of owed pay. I knew he was having it rough. So I went seventeen weeks without any pay. But I didn't expect him to bomb out on me. And he did. I trusted him, and I shouldn't have, I guess.

Well, the car was half mine. And he had a loan from a finance company. So I borrowed money from a brother to buy my own race car. Make it legal. I parked it in the front yard and worked at a dealership for almost a complete year, the rest of '67. That was in Kenosha, Wisconsin.

That's when some friends of mine who worked for American Motors came to me and asked me could I make a race car out of an American Rambler. I said, "Yeah, I probably could make a race car out of it."

I got more and more involved in it. I became the driver and pretty soon the engineer and the mechanic. It got to be a blast, the thing really worked. And I won third in championship points with a little American Rambler.

That was when the big Trans-Am thing was going on. American Motors, Ford, and Chevy and so forth. I submitted a proposal to American Motors to run a Trans-Am team for them in 1968. But I didn't get it. The fellow that did, though, called me and said, "Everywhere I go, I keep hearing your name in American Motors. I'd like to meet you." So I went down and talked to him and went to work for him. I had one condition, though. They already had contracted drivers. That was Pete Revson and George Follmer. So I said, "I'll go to work on one condition. If either driver's seat is ever open, I'm the next driver or I'm gonna quit."

I went to work and did most of the designing and engine building. In '68 George Follmer couldn't show up for a race. I thought, Here's my chance. I asked if I could qualify the car. They said I could.

Well, I had Pete on the pole already. So I thought the only way I'll keep this ride for the weekend is if I bump Pete over and I set on the pole. And like fifteen minutes before the end of qualifying, I went out, took a deep breath, and knocked 1.6 seconds off the track record. I set on the pole, knocked Pete over. So I had both American Motors cars in the front row. Which was beautiful. It was the first time they'd ever been in the front row.

In 1969 American Motors held driver interviews out at the Stardust track in Las Vegas. I spent most of the day strapping all the drivers in and telling them how the car worked and all that stuff, giving everybody a fair shot. So now, after the car was half worn out, they said they'd give me an opportunity. I said either I get the driving job or I'm going to quit. I went out and set the fastest time of the whole weekend.

So here I was the driver, test driver, the fabricator, the engine builder, the whole works. And it was beautiful. I loved it. I lived it, you know, twenty-four hours a day. And then in late '69 American Motors and I had a disagreement. They wanted to know why they weren't winning races. And I told them why. I was leading races and things would break, stuff that I predicted. You know, you have victory right in front of you and things break, it's bad for your mind. Anyway, I split with American.

I was very disappointed. And then a week later my father passed away. And just, boom boom, everything hit so hard. I just kind of withdrew. I started driving outlaw. Just make up a name and go drive in super modifieds on some of those outlaw tracks. Not for money especially. I'd made good money. I had no money problems.

I'd called myself Jack Martin or Joe Martin. I always used the name Martin. And I drove like I didn't care if I lived or died. It's amazing how much you can win that way. I was depressed. I really was. All the hours I'd put in and . . . I figured I kind of got used. Everybody at American Motors was trying to save their hide. And so it ended up on me.

In 1970 I drove in the Continental series for Formula-A cars, finishing eleventh in the championship standings. In this series, my first in the Continental, I finished eight of the eleven races I started in the top ten—five of these in succession.

In the latter part of 1970 I set up permanently in Long Beach, California, and decided to try the USAC championship trail in 1971.

The way my career has gone—I became a good mechanic because that was the only way to become a good driver. That was my way of working my way up. The driving ability seemed to come naturally. The hardest part was being able to be in the right car at the right place. That was the hard part.

Those early years racing was everything. One hundred percent. Nobody or nothing came before it. I was selfish with my time. I couldn't spend the kind of time I should have with a lotta people.

Sometimes I worked three, four days and nights in a row to get a car prepared to go run a race. No sleep. In the late '60s, it was nothing abnormal for me to work three days and nights, never shut it down. About three days—and then I'd get tired and I'd sleep maybe for twelve hours. And then get up and go again. I'd live out of my station wagon, preparing a car in different locations.

When I went on the USAC championship trail, I was just as caught up with it. When I came out to Long Beach, California, I had a race car and a trailer and a pickup. A friend of mine had a little place down on the peninsula. He said to me, "If you need a place to stay, you can stay with me until you get yourself squared away." Well, for a year I slept on the floor in front of the fireplace.

In 1971 I went to Indy for the first time. I went there with a normal-aspirated Chevy, a three-hundred-and-twenty-inch Chevrolet that we put in the Brabham car. I guess it's still the fastest normal-aspirated Chevy that ever ran at Indy. I think we ran around 165 after my rookie test. Then, soon as I took the rookie test, we put in an old Offy engine and I think it ran about 170 miles per hour.

I decided that 171 or 172 would make the show that year. But I didn't feel that I was ready to do it. A fellow who ended up a friend of mine, Dick Simon—he got bumped, and I turned it over to him to drive. At that time I didn't think I should attempt it. I thought Dick could run 171 miles per hour easier than I could, without risk to equipment and machinery. See, that's what's a little different about my setup. Most drivers just drive the car. But I own it, and so I have to be concerned about keeping it in good shape.

As always, it had to do with finances. I couldn't risk the

car by practicing a lot on it. And the practice was what I needed if I was going to try to qualify it myself. So I made the decision that Dick Simon was going to run it. I figured I had the best part of my racing career in front of me, and I didn't want to put it behind me. In the end, though, Dick Simon didn't get to try. The magneto went out on the starting line. And by the time we got it changed—just as we fired the engine—the gun went off. So we missed qualifying completely. Run out of time.

It was a setback. But no big deal, really. I never doubted I was going to succeed at Indy. It was always a matter of just how am I going to do it.

I did it the next year [1972] in a four-year-old Brabham. Surprised a lot of people by putting it into the fourteenth starting spot at Indy. [Martin finished sixteenth in the race.] And in the spring of '73 we bought the car from McLaren that Peter Revson had driven the year before.

We went through the car, changed the color and everything. We went to Indy with it, and we were the ninth fastest in the history of Indianapolis. In fact we were quicker than McLaren was with their car. Which was quite a kick. My so-called shoe-string operation beating out the big-money boys. The car also went 2, 3 miles an hour quicker than Pete had the year before.

That was the year of the crash—'73—and I was pretty involved in that crash. In fact, after I got out of the fire and everything, I figured that was it. There's no way the car was going to be able to run the next day when they started the race again. But with the help of everybody—and even the McLaren team came into the garage and gave me a hand—at four or five o'clock the next morning, I was finishing lining up the suspension. We just put everything back in shape, just bent it back into shape, using pop rivets to get it right.

I slept two hours before the race and was pretty well beat. They were going to start the race again the next day. So we got on the line, and I thought everything was pretty good, though I didn't have any idea of what the car was going to feel like. So just before they say, "Gentlemen, restart your engines," I checked all the pedals and stuff, and I pushed down the brake pedal. It went *kpow*, right to the floor. So I called the chief mechanic over, and I told him what was wrong. What happened in the fire the day before —it had melted the brake line, and it deteriorated enough that when I put brake pressure on it, it popped open. So I had no brakes.

So I said to my mechanic, "If there's any way possible I'm gonna stop this race. It looks like it's gonna rain; maybe it'll start raining any minute, and we can get this race stopped." I said, "Meanwhile have the wrenches ready. And when I come in, I'm gonna be waving like a maniac. Pay no attention to it, just grab the car, stop it. And put that brake liner on."

We started up. I was very careful not to get close to anybody 'cause I had no brakes. Then on corner three, I saw a drop of rain on the visor. I thought: This is it. I've got to stop this race. I gotta stop this race. So I come in, and by that time Mr. Harlan Fengler and everybody . . . they don't know whether to start the race or stop it or what.

So I came in waving my arms and wiping my face, pointing up to the skies, saying, "You're crazy. It's raining." And I pulled into the pit. Well, they thought I'd just quit running because it was raining. So they waved it red, and that saved us on the start. See, I thought I could help him make the decision to stop this race. So we were in the pits fixing the brakes and watching. They were getting the cars regrouped. They were looking at the sky. So we're on the point of being ready when, sssshhhhh, it rained. I said, "Push it in the garage."

So we made an external brake line. And we started to race the next day. Then Swede Savage had his crash. We had to restart the race once more. And when they finally stopped the race, I was in for eighth place. Which isn't bad for a shoe-string operation, so-called. And it beats standing behind a plow.

salt walther

SALT WALTHER is a cocksure driver who races
at Indy in cars owned by his industrialist father,
George Walther. In spite of that apparent advantage
Salt has not had an easy time of it.

My father is George Walther, Junior. In the early 1960s he took over as president of Dayton-Walther Corporation [a company making products for the transportation industry]. At that time the company was selling ten million dollars in products a year. Today the same firm is making more than one hundred and fifty million dollars annually.

Since 1955 my father has entered cars at Indy. Among the drivers he's hired over the years are Juan Manuel Fangio, Troy Ruttman, Peter Revson, Johnny Rutherford, Dick Simon, Carl Williams, to name a few.

My given name is David Walther. But people call me Salt. I've been around racing as long as I can remember. One year in the late 1950s Mike Magill was driving for Dad and got hurt. His car hit the wall and flipped over. And Dad brought him back to Dayton, Ohio, where we live. Dad personally took care of him. Brought him back to the house. Put him in the guest room.

Before he came to the house, though, he was in the hospital. And I got to see him. I remember thinking, "That man will never live." Mike was a helluva mess. The crash ground off part of his head. But he made it out of the hospital.

One night I woke up in the middle of the night. I don't sleep worth a damn. And I looked out the window. Here's Mike. All by himself. Walking up and down the driveway. And I asked Dad the next day, "What's Mike doing? What's he doing walking up and down the driveway?" Dad said Mike felt like he had snakes crawling all over him. He just had to get up and walk around for a while.

Since 1972 I've been driving for Dayton-Walther at

Indy. And I know what people say. "His daddy bought him a ride." Or, "Boy, the Walthers spend a helluva lot of money to get in the show."

My reaction is, *Yes, Dad's got money. He worked his tail off for it, too. And any way he wants to spend it, that's his business. If people don't like it, the hell with 'em.*

The first that most people heard of Salt Walther was my second Indy race—1973. That was the year Swede Savage was killed, and there was a spectacular crash at the start of the race. My car was the one that was at the center of the crash. Spectators were hurt by flying debris. Cars got bent up. And I was seriously injured.

What happened—what people saw—was my car hit a tire on Jerry Grant's Eagle and flip high into the air. For a moment it was up in the air and then it spun sideways and came down on fire. It was like a blanket of fire on the track. Other cars were losing parts. Some of the pieces flew up in the stands. My car hit another and then spun down the track with the wheels off it.

That's what people saw. A lot of fans—and drivers too—said that Walther blew it. They said it was my fault. I remember, though, that when they pulled me out of the car right after it happened, they asked me first, what was my name? Second, where was I? And third, what happened? I told 'em I was at the Indy 500. My name was Salt Walther. I was a helluva mess at the time but still conscious. And I told 'em: "Goddammit, somebody hit me from behind."

I've seen the movies of that start hundreds of times since. Andy Granatelli gave me the film of the race. It came out in the papers that I said that maybe I *didn't* get bumped. I never said that. I never will say it. I was bumped. Plain and simple. You slow down the film and there's no other conclusion you can come to.

In that crash forty percent of my body was burned. Parts of my kneecap were smashed. My left hand was burned so bad that the tips of all the fingers were amputated. My other hand—the fingers are at different angles to each other, which you don't really notice most of the time 'cause the hand's not spread open in ordinary circumstances. Over the left hand I wear a glove, a black glove.

When I finally did come back to racing, the other drivers didn't coddle me about what I'd been through. One driver, when he saw me, made a claw of his hand and, with that warped fist, waved and said, "Hi, how are you?" Billy Vukovich called me after I'd been out of the hospital a while and said, "We just want to tell you we just inducted you into the Crispy Critter Club."

By then, hell, I could laugh about it. For a while, though, it was touch and go. I was in the Michigan Burn Center for two and a half months. They were going to cut off the left hand at first, but the doctor felt he could save it. I had a lot of skin grafts on it.

When somebody's hurt, he goes through a helluva rehabilitation process. I had to learn to walk again. When they got me up to walk, I'd get dizzy and go sit back down. Then they had two big fellas, two great big fellas, come in and lift me up and hold me in the air and let me try and move my legs. But I didn't have enough muscles to do anything. I couldn't walk at all.

I remember the first time I saw what I looked like. This was after I'd begun to walk on my own. There was a mirror over the sink in the bathroom. And I looked in it. And I saw myself and, honest to God, didn't believe it was me. I couldn't believe it was that bad. I had no brows and almost like a burr haircut. And I was wasted. I'd lost fifty pounds or so.

I was astounded. I didn't cry 'til I got back to the bed. I think I cried for about two minutes. Then I thought: Well, shit. This isn't going to do any good either. But for a while I was very depressed.

When I finally got out, I was still weak. And I set to work to build myself up. For my hands I got a box of sand. I'd splash on some rubbing alcohol, which toughens the skin. Splash on the alcohol and take a handful of sand and squeeze and squeeze it. Then I progressed to hand grips.

When I first got out, I remember I put on my nice-looking crepe slacks and my good-looking shirts. And I looked like a skeleton walking in them because they didn't come close to fitting. I mean, I was skinny. Eventually I began to work with the weights.

See, that's where I was so fortunate. I've been lifting weights since I was sixteen years old. And you know, hell, I was a damn good athlete. One of the top athletes probably in the country. But after the wreck I looked like I was fifteen years old again. A scarecrow.

Before I raced cars I raced boats. I started racing them when I was thirteen. My father was a champion boat racer. He raced outboard and inboard hydroplanes.

When I was even younger, I thought nothing of taking my father's motorcycle—he had a little Harley—and go off and ride it around the neighborhood. Several times, when I was, oh, maybe seven, eight years old, the cops stopped me and brought me back.

Naturally, I'd take the Harley when Dad wasn't around. I rode it all the time when he was gone. I thought he didn't know. But later I realized he must have. Because the thing was always full of gas.

Anyway, a bunch of times the cops stopped me. 'Cause the neighbors would call and say the little bastard's at it again. Pretty soon, I graduated to the Broadslider. It was an old beat-up car with wheelbarrow tires and wheels and a real motor. It would run about 35, 38 miles per hour, which is quick when you're just a kid. Back then, my brothers and I used to have a path we made that ran around the property. And my brothers and I took it out on the path, and you could just slide it and slide it.

Later, when I was in high school, I still went in for that sort of thing. I was in a fraternity in high school . . . had beautiful black pins . . . everything. We had a big party. There was a steep hill nearby. We bought skateboards, and we'd go down the hill. You might get running 40 miles an hour, which is pretty damn quick. And when you fell, it would just tear you all to pieces. You'd slide. It was like falling off a bicycle going 40 miles an hour. Just tears you all to hell.

And I thought, well, it wasn't fast enough. So I got a ski rope, tied it on the back of a car, held on to it, and stood on this skateboard. Hell, I was traveling along about 70 and fell off the damn thing. Tore all the skin off my arms, my elbows.

About that time we also had a race course in the fields back of the house. The course was a quarter of a mile around. We bought a '55 Chevy. And my brothers and I would get running maybe 80 miles an hour on this quarter mile. I turned it over about eight times. Car's still sitting down there today. You can see it from the bedroom window. I got twenty-five acres right behind the house.

In fact you can see a bunch of cars down there. A '55 Ford. A '55 Chevy. A '56 Ford truck. Some others. They're just total rust wrecks. There's nothing left of them. They've been sitting there since 1960-something. Those days we'd throw a few bucks apiece into a pot and race for that. Serious racing. We'd take turns. Get a stopwatch and time it.

Today, we still race 'round the property here. In the off-season. You get, say, five guys or so, come over. In the garage I've got three-wheel racers. And it's understood that anyone that bends one up pays for it. But you take the pick of any of the five you want.

We even race at night. I can light up the track. There are lights all around the house. Plus, I took the light out of the pool and set it on the diving board. It's a four-hundred-watt light, and it lights up the whole back of the yard. With these three-wheelers, it'd be like driving a stock car damn near . . . on a small course. They handle like a car, these three-wheelers do. The way they're set up.

In high school I'd take my motorcycle and get it up on its rear wheel and ride it like hell past this place where everybody hung out. I'd go out there 'cause I liked to show off. And I'd get it up on its wheel and just ride the damn thing down through there. And I'd spin it out and just have a good time.

Sometimes I fooled around with the cops with my car. One time I pulled right up in front of a cop at a restaurant, hit the accelerator, spun it around in a figure eight, and went like hell. And the cop couldn't catch me. Those cop cars wouldn't run like my car would.

He followed me all the way here to the house. And I got out with another fellow. We were both in the car. He said he was going to give us a ticket. And naturally he gave it to me. I said, "Well, I wasn't driving."

See, it was a Corvette and I'd had a—what the hell you call it?—a sunscreen in it. At that time, it was the "in" thing. It made the windows look dark blue. And the thing is that a policeman has to be able to identify you. He obviously knew the car, but he couldn't identify me as the driver.

As a kid I worked. I worked hard. My father had a marina. I was a mechanic for five years—built outboard motors. Redid boats that came in, refinished them.

I worked around the house too. Cut the grass, cleaned the johns. I paved the driveway by myself.

Not that I was the model son. I wasn't. Even though my dad was loaded, for a while I used to run around with some real bums. Always getting into trouble. In fact there was a time my father threw me out of the house. I deserved it. I was too cocky, too smart for my own good.

The thing he really couldn't abide, though, was my habit of getting into fights. I used to get into a lot of fights. For a time I just liked to fight.

I still get into fights. Not that I look for them. But I don't back off either. I may not be the roughest guy in the country. But I'm no pushover. If I get into a fight, somebody knows he's going to get a good one.

Like this ring finger. See how the knuckle's busted. I broke it a few years ago at Indy.

We were at a bar one night, partying. And everybody was having a good time. I was dancing with a pretty good-

looking girl. Damn well endowed. Built real sharp. Some guy came over, said, "Look at those boobs."

And he said it two, three times. Finally I said, "Hey, shove off." He just kept shooting his mouth off. And then he told me to watch my mouth, and pushed me.

That's when I nailed him. And down he went. He needed about ten stitches over his eye. Trouble was, I ended up breaking my knuckle. I hit like a mule when I hit, but I end up breaking my wrist or knuckle. I always do that.

But see, if you're not built well or you're meek and quiet, people don't say a helluva lot. But any time that they think you've got something or they think you're a big deal, people are bound to be jealous. I mean, you know if you're good-looking or if you're not. I'm not trying to be cocky or mouthy, but I know I'm a decent-looking guy. I'm not a slob. And it just seems like somebody's always looking to shoot his mouth off.

I'd see it with Peter Revson, too. I knew Peter. Peter would always walk away. I saw people say a lot of stuff about Peter. They'd refer to him as Mr. Money. Or Mr. Sophisticate. That gets tiresome after a while.

People have strong reactions to me. Whether they know me or not. Even when I was racing boats, I'd get hate mail from strangers. Letters that would say, "You're gonna get killed in that boat, and it'll be the best thing that ever happened 'cause you're too cocky and you're living on your dad's money." That kind of mail.

The funny thing, though, is I never got one like that signed. People who write that sort of letter tend to be anonymous. They hide behind their anonymity.

After the crash I got many letters. Mostly they were nice ones. People who were concerned about my injuries. There was one family in Iowa that wrote me every day. The Crofts. Wrote me every day and sometimes sent me nice things. Very fine people.

But I'd be lying to you if I told you I didn't get some hate mail too. Pretty sick stuff. I got one letter that said that now that I had scars all over me and was disfigured for life and looked like hell, I might as well just die in the hospital.

That wasn't all either. The letter said that if by chance I recovered, the writer of the letter would, by God, make sure I died some time shortly after my release from the hospital.

Like I say, though, that doesn't bother me. I'm used to it. Hell, even as a race driver, I've been in a few tiffs too. One time it was with [Bill] Vukovich. Like you might have heard that Vuky gave Rutherford the finger the first year that John won the race. Well, he damn sure did. He gave me the finger, too. He was running quicker than I was. Every so many laps he'd be coming up, coming behind me where he'd be able to pass. Well, I figured if he's quick enough, get around me. If not . . .

I moved one way to let him around. And he thought I was going the other way. So he got a little bit sideways and damn near had an accident. He came by me later and gave me the finger. Out on the speedway. And I was just madder than hell. After the race I got out of the car and walked up to him. I said, "Bill, what is this with you giving me the finger?"

He just yelled, "YOU WANNA MAKE SOMETHING OF IT WHERE EVERYBODY CAN HEAR ABOUT IT? THIS ISN'T THE PLACE TO TALK ABOUT IT." And everybody turned around.

I know how Billy gets. But I was . . . I was still pretty hot too. I didn't say anything, though, because I know how Billy is. And he knows how I am. We both have hot tempers.

When I first came out of the hospital after recovering from the crash, I looked like a skeleton. Or a scarecrow—to see the way my clothes fit me.

I didn't have any arms, or anything. I just couldn't believe it.

I left the hospital and went home in the Dayton-Walther

company plane. I couldn't even get up the steps to the plane. Had to be helped up.

I remember Dad buckled the seat belt, and he hit my hand when he was trying to buckle it, and I yelled "Dammit!" Oh, it hurt.

But what I remember was that when we got back home, I wanted to see the car. The race car. It was down at my dad's marina.

So we went there. The car was in the new race-car shop we were building then. I saw the car. I knew then I'd be back driving again.

Then I went home. That night I drove my own car, a Cadillac. It had been sitting in the garage for about three months. I had to be helped to get the car started, of course. But I drove it home. I had to call Dad to help me get back into the house. I just ran out of steam.

But there was never any question in my mind that I was going to try to drive a race car again. I came back to racing the year after the crash. My hands, of course, were not exactly the same. There are certain nerves that aren't there.

Still and all, it's better than it was way back when. In those days my fingers were totally frozen solid and bent down. The joints didn't work. It took a while just slowly moving them and working with them. Finally I got to where I could move them.

At the end of every single finger now there's no meat. It's just bone sticks. It's covered with skin, obviously. But there's no meat on it. The hands were badly burned. Some nerves were severed. I have very little feeling in the bad hand.

But I'll tell you this. I have more strength in this hand than you've got in both your hands. You won't believe it. Lemme show you something. Turn that recorder off. Gimme your arm a minute. [Walther proceeds to squeeze the interviewer's arm with his gloved hand.] That's without doing it hard. I've got unreal strength. 'Cause I do chin-ups and all that.

The first time I got back into the car was at Ontario.

Goodyear was running tire tests. I was so damn nervous that I thought I'd throw up before I got going. I seldom get nervous. My ankles were still swelling, getting sore. And that's where a lot of the work is done—in the ankles.

That was just part of it. I still had my legs wrapped with gauze up to my butt. The skin continued to crack, and bleed. But I had to do it now and make sure I was going to be able to.

My left hand was still sore. It was still giving me trouble. I had handgrips put onto the steering wheel because I didn't have the strength in either hand. But I had handgrips so my hands wouldn't slip. 'Cause a little slip, over you go.

I thought I might run five or six laps, and maybe the nerves would quit. And all of a sudden I'd be into the wall. So I took all the precautions I could.

I remember that my hands were sweating so bad. My gloves are leather gloves, and they were both wet. By the time I finished they were both wet.

Sure, I was scared. Would you want to get back in a car after you busted your butt in it? It always goes through your head that you're taking a chance of getting hurt.

But I got out there, and in twenty laps I ran 187 miles an hour. That made me the fastest car the first day and the second fastest the second day. And the second fastest the third day. We locked it up and came home. I showed myself I could do it. I had the reflexes back. I had the eyesight. I had everything going for me. Now it was a matter of being able to take three hours worth of racing in one of those cars.

The thing that really tickled me was that I showed a lot of people that said I was not going to be able to drive again that I could. That's what really tickled me.

johnny parsons

JOHNNY PARSONS grew up close enough to the
Indianapolis Speedway to hear the roar of
racing engines as a schoolboy in class. He is the son
of a former Indy 500 winner, a relationship
that added pressure to his own career.

I grew up in California and Speedway, Indiana. As a kid, I used to hear adults whisper, "That's Johnnie Parsons's kid." And I'd feel just a little embarrassed by the attention.

My father, Johnnie Parsons, won the Indianapolis 500 in 1950. He won it in a yellow Kurtis-Kraft. That year he and Mauri Rose swapped the lead four times in the first two hundred and seventy-five miles. The third time Rose went past him my father passed him right back. And as he passed, he waved to the crowd. At least that's what I've been told.

My name is John Wayne Parsons. My father's middle name is Woodrow. Mom wanted a middle name for me that began with *W*. And at the time I was born the movie actor John Wayne was shooting a film at an abandoned airstrip near Newhall, California, my birthplace.

Coincidentally, when my first born, Johnny III, was born in 1966 in Encino, John Wayne was at the hospital waiting for the delivery of a daughter. And my boy arrived about twenty minutes before his gal. My mother-in-law told John Wayne that I was named after him and that the third would be named after him too. And he thought that was pretty good.

I didn't see much of my father because my parents separated when I was young. My mother married another driver, Duane Carter, Senior, whose sons, Pancho and Dana, are also professional race-car drivers.

I was always conscious of auto racing. I have memories of hearing the 1950 Indy 500 over the radio at my grandmother's house in Newhall. After that I don't remember too much about my father's career except for the day he was hurt badly in a crash at a half-mile dirt track in the

LA area. It was the worst accident he'd ever had. He dislocated both shoulders, required more than one hundred stitches under one of his arms, had a concussion and broken ribs. He was busted up pretty good. I remember how worried people were.

In Speedway, Indiana, Pancho, Dana, and I lived in a house on Fourteenth Street. We used to go to a baseball field and drive our quarter midgets around the bases. We did a lot of things as kids that were race-oriented. Like we took our bicycles out when school was over and raced them around the grammar school and clocked each other with stopwatches. It was regular play to us. It was not forced on us. It was just fun.

As a kid I competed on a little quarter midget track. The first time was out by Pomona, east of Los Angeles. My first ride the tie rod broke. The tie rod controls both front tires and coordinates the steering. The tires were going different directions at the same time, and I didn't know what was going on. I just kept standing on it—you know, driving like hell.

My mother noticed I was getting out of the groove, which is the strip of rubber laid down on the track by cars coming through the corner. Finally she stepped over a hay bale and motioned me to move down in the groove. She didn't know my tie rod was broken. She thought it was my error. In fact in her concern for my finding the groove she damn near got hit by the car when I went off the end of the track and through the hay bales into a chain-link fence.

My mother's name is Arza. She used to go with us to the quarter-midget races my brothers and I were in. She kind of worked on the cars and pushed us off. And she was our chief mechanic, you might say. She knows cars. Even today she's got a toolbox in the back of her car.

I remember when Dana first tried a quarter midget. He was about four years old. My stepfather, Duane, had told us how to get the thing stopped. But with the car vibrating and noisy, Dana probably just forgot.

He figured, though, that if he steered right at his father,

his father would make the car stop. Which is what Dana did. It was some sight. It looked as though Dana was chasing him or trying to run him down. Before that could happen, Duane Senior stepped over a log, and Dana ran his car into the log and slowed down enough so that his father could stop it. I tell you, we all just set down and rolled over laughing. It was like Duane had a string behind him towing a quarter midget.

All of us—Dana, Pancho, and me—got along pretty well. Maybe there were occasional flare-ups. Tell you the truth, though, I don't really remember them. What I do remember is an incident that happened between Pancho and me at Pocono once. Pancho lost control of the car and got in my car a little bit. Cost me some money and cost the car owner some money. I talked to him about that.

As for the fact that my father was a former Indy winner, the adults made more of it than the kids. Kids don't think too much about things like that. If they like you, they like you. If they don't, they don't. It doesn't have anything to do with who your father is.

There's a funny story with my first passenger car. I had a '52 Ford. One night when I was coming home from a date, the brakes went. I had the traffic lights synchronized, though. So I was able to make it home. About a block from home I downshifted. I turned the key off. I was going to pull in the parking slot next to the house, with the front end of the car facing the house. I had figured that at four or five miles an hour, I'd bump this low curb and that would effectively stop the car.

I miscalculated. It didn't stop the car. Thirty feet more, I was going to be right in the living room. I had to make a sharp left down the driveway and aim for the garage. The garage door just kept getting bigger and bigger. I took the garage door down and piled all the bicycles and soapboxes up in the back of the garage and made one big hell of a noise. Scared our poor dog as well. All of which prompted me to get into the mechanics of my passenger car.

One way or another, I was always involved with cars. In high school, I worked at a speed shop on Sixteenth Street and Main Street in Speedway and a gas station right across from the Motor Speedway.

I enjoyed working in the speed shop 'cause it gave me a chance to fool around a little bit with the race cars that were in the shop. Sometimes I'd go out on the midget circuit and stooge. You know, change tires, push the car off. I got to see racing behind the scenes, and it got me more interested.

I saw the good and bad both. There was one driver I worked for, a very big name—a former Indy winner, in fact—who did something to me as a kid I guess I've never forgiven him for. This was quite a few years ago. I was still in high school. One night I went downtown to a movie on a double date. We're standing in line. And here was the driver and his wife. I said hello to him and went to introduce him to my date. After all, this is a guy I work for, he's a hot-dog Indy driver and everything. Before I had a chance, though, to introduce him, he says, "Oh, there's that Parsons kid. He sweeps my floors."

I was stunned. I didn't know what to say. Ever since, I've been turned off on the guy. I don't think he realized what effect it could have. I've had an education by having children of my own. The older you get, the more you tend not to realize what goes through a younger person's head. You've got to be careful what you say to younger people.

But that experience was an exception. Most of the times I had with the drivers were fun. I remember one USAC midget driver they called Wormie. Called him Wormie because he was what drivers called goosie. He was jumpy, nervous. He was a little guy and kind of talkative, out-going. One race, Wormie's car got into another guy's car. And afterward, the fellows were kidding him that the other guy was looking to whack him around.

Well, Wormie wasn't called Wormie for nothing. I guess the prospect of what this guy might do to him got him more tense than usual. Because when one of the fellows, fooling around, goosed him, it was one helluva sight. His arms flew up, he looked as though he was about to go into orbit. We all fell out, laughing.

Johnny
Parsons

96

I began racing on weekends. At first I held a job as a fork-lift operator. I did that for several years.

I began thinking, though, about police work. As a kid, I'd always been curious about it. I remember walking past the patrol car and hearing the radio going and wondering what the guys were doing, how their system worked.

I went ahead and took the test and went to police academy. They really worked you there. Pushed you physically, mentally. Most of the guys in our class were back from Vietnam. In a lot of ways, they said, the training was very similar to boot camp.

Except we got to go home at night. We used to run seven miles a day. They also marched us through tear gas. I was in great shape. The only other time I was in that kind of shape was my final year on the high school wrestling team.

In 1967 I became a police officer with the Los Angeles Police Department. As a rookie I was involved in a high-speed chase that turned out to have curious origins. We were in a pursuit on Santa Monica Boulevard, around a four-block-square area of Santa Monica, LaGrange, and a few other streets.

What my partner and I saw was a car and a pickup truck to its rear running at a high rate of speed. The front car wouldn't pull over until the pickup truck did.

We emerged from the police cruiser. A male was in the car, and he was with a woman. Right away, he says, "Don't let her near me. Don't let her near me," referring to the woman in the pickup truck behind him. We threw the cuffs on him and questioned all parties concerned. This is what happened:

It seems the male was at an office party, and he'd taken off with one of the secretaries. He took off just as his common-law wife showed up with their pickup truck.

And as he was driving away, she drilled the back of his car —ran right into it. And off they went, with her in hot pursuit. He wasn't about to stop until she did. He figured she was going to kill him.

I raced half midgets and three-quarter midgets for a while. Finally I decided to try a full midget car. I went up to a race in Santa Maria, looking for a ride. I sat around the sign-in area. And finally this guy shows up with a so-so car. But as a rookie I wasn't going to be fussy. I was looking the midget over when I saw the owner ask the officials a question. The officials pointed toward me. I stepped right up and asked could I drive his car. He stalled me to see if a more established driver might show up. Meantime, I'm helping him unload and talking to him about the car, trying to sound intelligent, like I knew what all the parts were for on the car. He says, "I'll tell you what, you go ahead and warm it up. If you look okay, we'll let you qualify it. If somebody else's engine blows, I'll let him run it." Fortunately no engines blew. And nobody crashed in warm-ups. So I qualified fourth fastest of thirty-five cars and did well in the races.

I figured I had a good thing with the guy. But he was, it turned out, not too reliable. Three times I showed up for races at Ascot Park, and he left me stranded each time. I'd be standing at the pit gate with my uniform on and my helmet bag in hand. The next day I'd call him, and he'd say, "Well, we didn't quite get it together in time." And the problem was, I found out, that the guy was hanging around the bars more than the garage. And I'd say, "Well, I'll come over and help you some time." And he'd say, "No. No. All it needs is this or that. I can do it in a half hour. Everything'll be cool." Never showed, though.

It was tough, just starting out, getting a ride. What you do is go around to the shops and garages or hang around the pit area and you talk to the owners. You make yourself available, let them know you're ready to go racing. And this is what I was doing.

Guys would say, "Well, we don't care who you are. It doesn't mean you're going to be a race driver like your old man. Go get some experience." They wanted to see me in somebody else's car first before they risked theirs. But I'd go to another car owner, and he'd say the exact same thing. It was a vicious circle.

You get angry. But you can't show it. I was trying to be kind of humble about the whole thing because I really wanted to race. And I figured if I really got mad and hollered and screamed at somebody, it wouldn't help.

Another thing was the cars. Some of them were real junk. In fact I had one where the brakes failed as I came in to pit during prerace practice at Ascot Park. There were people in the pits everywhere. And there were cars plugged up at the other end of the pits, waiting to get on to the track.

I knew I was gonna hit something. To the right were pickup trucks getting ready to push off the next group of cars. They were waiting like taxis do at the airport. If I went under one of those, I could take my head off. Then there were groups of people standing around. I didn't want to run over any of them. I just had to pick out something to run into and crash. I was only going 40 miles per hour and knew I was gonna be okay as long as I didn't hit a pickup truck.

I picked the tail of a race car. I tried to pick out what we call a shit box, an inferior car. I hit it. It jumped over and bumped somebody in the leg, just cut him a little bit. Didn't hurt him. He didn't require hospital time. So I came out of it okay.

Right away, though, people started blaming me for it. And that set me to hollering. See, I was scared and angry both. I was hollering and screaming at the car owner. Which was a change. Before that I was afraid to say a word to him.

In '68 the Los Angeles Police Department had a tactical alert when Martin Luther King was assassinated.

At the time I had a throat infection and was officially on sick leave. I didn't go to work. But I did race, even though I had a strep throat. And I won the race. The news of it was in the papers. My watch commander saw it and called me on the phone. He said, "Go get a return-to-duty slip and come back and see me in the office." And so I went to get a return-to-duty slip, but they wouldn't give it to me because I wasn't well yet.

When I finally did get well and go back, the watch commander gave me ten days off. He suspended me for ten days because he figured if I'm sick and not able to work on the Police Department, I should stay home. And right then and there, things were becoming very conflicting.

I had a month's vacation and came back to Indy with my wife and kids. And I looked around for a sprint-car ride. Went over to a practice session in Winchester, which is the scariest track in the country. And this other rookie whose dad used to race a little bit was trying to get the ride also. So the owner of the car let us both take the car out and practice. The other guy spun it down on the first turn. I lost it coming off turn four. The car was really junk. But you have to get started in something.

Anyway, here's the point of the story. Before I got in the car, the owner said, "Well, how many races have you run in California?" And I told him, well, that I'd been running midgets and three-quarter midgets and did this and that in midgets and this and that in three-quarters. And he said, "How about sprint cars?" And I said, "Oh heck, I've been running sprint cars for about two years." [Smiles.] Which wasn't the case at all. I'd never been in a sprint car.

But in this sport—and it doesn't matter if your dad was a former Indy 500 winner like mine was—an owner wants an experienced guy. So I knew if I said I hadn't run any sprint cars, he would say why don't you come back when you get the experience in somebody else's car. And there was no way I was going through that again, like I'd done in the midgets. So I got the damn ride.

It's that way all the way up the line, the Indy cars as well. Everybody's hustling to get a ride. And again, like you hear we second-generation guys have it easier. . . . Well, that's not so. I remember one time Tassi Vatis promised me a ride in his Indy car at Pocono. And he said, "You'll probably get to run it at Pocono. Come on over and get there early so you can take your test early and everything."

I got there. A lot of guys were hustling around, trying to get that ride. Veteran drivers who didn't have a ride and who were determined to scare one up. I found out later that one of those veterans had been down to the officials complaining that they shouldn't give me a chance to take a rookie test, and he was talking to Tassi Vatis, the car owner, and telling him that I was gonna crash his car and I wasn't a good driver, which really upset me. And the guy shut me out of that ride. 'Cause he talked Vatis into letting *him* run it instead.

Eventually, I decided to go all out at racing. I resigned from the LAPD. Some of the officers—the sergeants and lieutenants—looked at me like there was something wrong with me. They couldn't conceive of anybody in police work giving it up. But, face it, racing was number one with me.

For me there's just no comparison to the thrill of running a race car. It's hard to put it in terms that a layman can understand. I remember, though, once reading an article that quoted Sterling Moss on the subject. He said it was just like an artist, a painter, putting the final stroke on a painting and saying, "There." For the driver, the checkered flag is the same sort of feeling. It's the equivalent of: "There."

So there were a few years where I raced midgets and sprint cars. I got experience. It was barely a living, though. The first couple of summers, I had to work for the railroad to pay the bills. As time went on, things got better.

I can remember the first sprint-car race I won. It was at New Bremen, Ohio, which is approximately seventy miles north of Dayton. The speedway there is a paved oval, a half mile around. I won the race, and I felt like I was floating.

Someone at the track brought out a case of beer. We celebrated. My stepfather, Duane Carter, was there. So was Pancho. Duane Senior was helping me from the infield, signaling how far ahead I was, that sort of thing. By the time we reached a truck stop, just inside the Indiana border, Duane fell on top of the hood of the car next to us. It was that good a celebration.

By 1972 I'd made it to championship cars. I drove my first one for Bill Finley at Milwaukee. The same year I qualified for the California 500 and ran eighty-eight laps before the car developed valve problems. I finished twenty-second in the race.

Naturally, as I moved up through the ranks, the fact that I was a second-generation driver was frequently referred to. Being second generation has its pros and cons. It helps you because you know a lot of the people from the news media. And you know some car owners and mechanics. But that doesn't necessarily mean you're going to be driving for these people.

It's hard on a young driver to be compared constantly with his father. There was a time I used to really get turned off because I'd hear it all the time. Always introduced as the son of a former Indy 500 winner. You get a bellyfull. Finally I just decided not to let it bother me.

The championship cars, what we call Indy cars, I found are more of a mental strain. 'Cause you know there's no margin for error. And it's harder to feel the car when you sit so far in front of the rear axle. In Indy cars you just have to concentrate more.

At certain tracks—I'm talking about ones like the Texas World Speedway in College Station and the Michigan International Speedway—the problem is compounded by neck strain that's caused by the high bank of the track. That's why the drivers wear a strap on their helmet that takes the pressure off the neck muscles. Sissy strap, some call it.

I'll tell you, though—the experience in dirt-track races gets a fellow used to physical strain. And more. Before we started using the full-face helmets, I got some fat lips on dirt tracks from rocks flying up. My dad, when he raced, used to hold a handkerchief in his teeth. It kept his teeth from getting knocked out by the rocks.

I use the handkerchief wrapped around my face to bite on sometimes. A tension reliever. I won't chew gum. Several years ago, a driver named Lee Kunzman smacked into the fence at Ontario. They got him to the infield hospital and were puzzled because he was turning blue. It turned out his chewing gum had lodged in his throat. It could have been very dangerous if somebody hadn't figured it out.

When I first started running midgets, I used to just about throw up. I'd get so nervous that I wouldn't perform well. I wasn't nervous about bodily injury. I was just too excited about the race.

That changes a bit as you become more experienced. Except, I guess, for Indy. Almost everyone reacts to Indy. I mean, you see some weird things before the race. Say like a guy who's a slow speaker will talk fast. Or a nice easygoing guy all of a sudden gets ticked off for no apparent reason. And everybody has to run off and go to the bathroom before the start of a race. Even if you went five minutes before.

For a race-car driver Indy is *the* place. I remember 1973, my first year there, I missed the show. When I realized I wasn't in the field, I went back to the garage in Gasoline Alley, locked the doors, sat under the rear wing with my back against the wall, and cried.

What a contrast the next year. The car wasn't quite right. But I wanted in bad. I took a pretty good chance of busting my butt in qualifying. It was my last shot. And I was pushing it. I felt just a bit out of control. The adrenalin was going. I just had to get it done. After the race I felt like a feather. Like I was floating. And I remember I was still vibrating. My hands were vibrating.

And that's what it's about. Trying to get the car to feel like part of your body. An extension. I get my mind into part of the machinery. And get it to be . . . like the tires are made of rubber, sure. But when things are right, you can feel the tires in your nerve ends. And when you take a car down into the corner as deep as it'll go and you know it's on the ragged edge, it's just like a shot in the arm. It's such a gratifying feeling that you've taken a piece of machinery and kind of glued yourself to it.

Johnny
Parsons

103

lloyd ruby

LLOYD RUBY drives against men half his age.
The slow-talking Texan's career dates back
to the late 1940s, a different racing era.

Wichita Falls, Texas, is where I'm from. I was raised there and live there now. It's oil country. Oil was discovered here at the turn of the century. Wichita Falls is one of the richest oil and natural-gas areas. Every direction you look, you see oil derricks and pumps.

It's flat wide-open country. I got to know it well on top of a motorcycle. We call 'em sickles. Riding sickles was an early love of mine. In fact the first time I fooled around with a racing car, part of my arm was in a cast from a sickle crash I'd been in.

Back then I worked in a sickle shop and raced them. In '46 they built a track here, called it the Speedrome. The fella that built it, Abe Rabin, had a car lot. I knew him, was around him a lot. So this one afternoon he was out there at the track playing with a midget car. I think he had about three or four of them. He asked me if I wanted to ride one.

Like I say, I had my left arm in a cast from a sickle crash. But it didn't really matter. I went ahead and played with the midgets that afternoon. And I thought it was a lotta fun.

Well, Abe saw that. And he asked me did I want to ride one in competition. Which I did—the next week in fact. I did pretty well. And I started doing it regularly for the rest of the season. We ran Wichita Falls; Lawton, Oklahoma; places like that.

At the end of the season I tallied up what I had won. It came to thirty-five hundred dollars. I said to myself: "This is better than working." I decided to see if I could be a driver.

Funny thing was that I wasn't intending to stay around Wichita Falls. I'd been up in Seattle, Washington, where my brother lived. I'd gone up there just to be going somewhere and ended up there for about eight, nine months. In Seattle I was working as a carpenter.

I came back to Wichita Falls just for a visit. I didn't intend to stay. But when I got hooked on the midgets, well, that changed my life around, I guess. Soon as that happened, I kept on working at the sickle shop and racing the midgets.

When I started racing 'round these parts, Rodger Ward was racing too. He started out driving for Abe Rabin too. Same as I did. Those days he was stationed at Sheppard Air Force Base, which is still in Wichita Falls and is the largest technical training system in the world.

Ward was a hard-driving young fella. You could almost count on him hitting the fence every night. He was the type of guy that always rode up high, and every once in a while he'd get up there pretty good.

The next year, 1948, I was running midgets in Texas and Oklahoma. Then I took off for New York. That was when they had the Polo Grounds, the baseball park. The New York Giants played there. They had a board track there that they moved in and out. First time it was ever run, I was there. Quarter-mile banked track. It had a real high bank. Stayed there about a year, then they moved it back to California.

My first races were on dirt. Running in Texas, it was dirt tracks. First time I run on asphalt was at Terre Haute, Indiana. It was a whole different style of driving. Same for boards. In dirt you go into a turn and you actually get the car sideways and then control it with your power to bring it on through the turns. In dirt you're in a kind of broadslide all the way through the turns. And especially if it's heavy dirt. On a board you get the least bit sideways, you just set there, and everybody goes by you.

First time in Terre Haute we were out there in the afternoon playing. And I was running that asphalt like I did dirt. And I thought I was getting 'round pretty good 'til this little Ford comes out there. It was what we'd call a junker. Fella driving it was going down there, stopping and going through the turns. And they said he was running pretty good. I thought, If they don't run any faster than that, well, hell. So while he was out there running, I go out. And what happened was he just run off and left me. 'Cause he was going through the turns straight, and I was going through them sideways. I learned right quick that you don't run it that way.

I was single in those days and making good money. In 1948 I was making one thousand, fifteen hundred dollars a week. And that sure beat working. After the war everybody had a little money, and they were looking for amusements, entertainment. And for a lot of them racing was it.

There was racing everywhere then. Indianapolis had racing six, seven times a week. I raced there for a while. Left Indianapolis, though, when the owner of the midget wanted to come back and run in Texas, Oklahoma, and Kansas. The owner was from that area and wanted to be around the car.

It was the same down there. All the racing a racing man could want. We'd travel about three thousand miles a week to race. At that time we were running Kansas City, Oklahoma City, Tulsa, Dallas, Houston. The trouble was that there wasn't the money here there was around Indianapolis. So I switched owners. I went back to the Indianapolis area.

Those days most of us stayed in Springfield, Illinois, for several days a week. 'Cause we were racing in that area. That was the place to stay. We'd stay there from Sunday night to Friday. Then we'd go to Indianapolis on Friday night. And Chicago on Saturday. Sundays, we'd race—oh, there was a place just outside of Springfield. And then we'd go on into Springfield for Monday.

Like I say, it was a boom time for us. Plenty of money. I'd hear the older fellas, the veteran drivers, talk of what it was like before the war ended. You'd hear stories about how a promoter would cut out with the money. The fellas from Dallas would talk about that happening. Two, three times it happened that way, they said. But I think in the long run, the fellas got more than their money out of it. Later on. [Laughs.]

Those were good days. Lotta fun. Kansas City, there'd be quite a few pranks up there. Back then the drivers were superstitious about peanuts. Peanuts were tabu. And there were a couple of drivers that would walk through the pits and just throw peanut shells in other guys' cars.

I don't know where that superstition came from. But the drivers were serious about it. Just like today a lotta drivers are superstitious about the color green. I guarantee you walk up to Foyt in a green shirt before the race and he'll . . . Like, at Pocono one year, when we run the midgets and sprint cars for this series they had, Foyt was getting ready to go, and there was a green truck fixing to push him off. And Foyt wouldn't let him. I mean, that's the only thing Foyt is superstitious on. Green.

Another thing that was big then was dropping firecrackers inside a race car while the driver was setting there. Just go up and catch a guy strapped in, seat belt and everything, and drop 'em in there. They were the kind that wouldn't hurt anybody. But it'd make a fella jump.

Back then I was more or less The Kid. But I was learning all the time, keeping my eyes open. On those tracks you picked up plenty of tricks. Like, a lot of times the West Coast drivers would be coming through here going to Indianapolis, Oklahoma, and so on. Troy Ruttman came through about '47, when he was really going strong. Come to Oklahoma City. And Oklahoma City was kind of a flat track. It was hard to pass. It was strictly what we call a pole track.

And Ruttman—he'd go up there, bump a guy and get him sidewise a little bit, and then drive on by him. Well, there was this here little fellow, driver name of Ted Parker, probably weighed about a hundred twenty, hundred twenty-five pounds. But he knew what he was doing.

Ted waved his finger at Ruttman. You know. Like, don't do it again. So about six or seven miles later Troy Ruttman found himself up in the grandstand because Ted Parker, he could do that and make you think you did it yourself.

I mean, all he did was just put on the brakes at the right time, you run over a wheel, and then you get airborne. He did it to Ruttman so easy, and I don't even think Troy knew what happened. But he did end up in the grandstand—it didn't hurt him, but I think it taught him a lesson.

Those days the sport was less organized. So there'd be more fistfights. Fellows get hot about the bumping, so forth. I had trouble. Was one fellow in Chicago. Had two or three fights with him. He was running midgets, he was going good. He took me out of the race two or three times. Bumped me. Well, this one time he took me out, I walked to the pits, and just about the time he was getting out of his car, I hit him. Knocked him down.

Now was another driver, Byron Fisher, a good friend of mine. He'd been having trouble with him too. Well, this fellow didn't know who'd hit him. And Byron was standing there—he thought it was Byron. So they started fighting. Byron finished the fight for me.

In Dallas a driver threatened me. And I happened to be friends with a Frenchman who drove. He was out of Dallas, a big tall Frenchman name of Marcel. He was a good man to have on your side. Marcel just walked over there—he usually carried a pretty good-sized knife—he just opened it up and told the fellow if he wanted to have any trouble, he'd take care of him first. [Laughs.]

They don't have the kind of action these days we had then. Like I say, we were running seven nights a week. Midget races now are . . . I doubt if they'll average over two a week. It'd be hard for a driver coming up to earn a living.

So much racing—rivalries were bound to happen. You still see it some. Drivers have trouble with each other. But not a whole lot. Most times now, it's the new drivers coming up. They're trying so hard that they get a little on the wild side. You have to call them down.

You'll talk to them after the race. And sometimes you'll talk to them during the race. On the track. Some drivers —they get going good—they think everybody ought to just move over for 'em.

I can remember when Andretti first got hot. Foyt talked to him at Phoenix. They were running about 160 miles an hour. And at that time Andretti was a little bit on the wild side when he was going good. Of course, Andretti—he'd been having troubles with two or three other drivers. Foyt's the one you don't fool with. 'Cause Foyt come up the hard way in the midgets and sprint cars, just like I did.

So at Phoenix they tangled. That's the way you talk to a fellow. Tangle on the track. What it was—Andretti just tried to cut him off going down a straightaway at Phoenix, and Foyt just stuck the wheel right into him. And they both went out.

Foyt got out of the car and was halfway over there to Andretti before he just stopped and turned around and went back. Because if he had ever got a hold of him, there's no telling what Foyt would have done to him. After that Andretti didn't give a whole lot of trouble to anybody. I mean, one lesson like that can wise you up right quick.

Running the midgets night after night you learn to protect yourself. When you run midgets, you run close. I mean, if a guy bumps you or tries to knock you out of the way, well, after a while you learn that you can stop that.

A lot of times a guy behind you—he'll bump you maybe once or twice. In other words when a guy in midgets bumps you, you can tell whether it's intentional or not. Like if he's really trying to get me out of the way, he'll catch me in the middle of a turn, or coming off a turn. You catch me just right, with just a nudge, you can get me sideways.

If a guy does that, you know it's intentional. You've got to keep the car straight. You've got to stay inside of him and more or less keep the car straight. Usually, after a guy does that so many times, especially back when we were running the midgets down here in Texas, that's when a fight would start. Or you would tangle on the track.

You'd do like Ted Parker did. Use your brakes. What you gotta do when you hit your brakes, you have to be straight. If you hit your brakes real hard, he's gonna hit you and go sideways. And he'll usually take himself out. 'Cause his first instinct is to try to miss you. And when he tries that, he's sideways and in trouble. And that's where he sits.

At that time you'd see quite a few fights in the pits. After a heat or a race you come in, and a driver would go over and have it out in the pits. Usually it wouldn't last too long because everybody around would try to stop it. But you'd always see some action about every two, three nights. These days, on the championship trail, you won't see hardly any fights anymore because there is a heavy fine against fighting. And it's considered bad for the grandstand, for the fans. But at times you'd still like to fight. [Laughs.]

Like nowadays, some people say Foyt's a bully. It's not my opinion, though. I'd rather race with him than anybody—I mean, real close competition. Because he'll always give you room. He might not give you much, but he'll give you enough room that you can make it. And that's more than I can say for a lotta the top drivers now that I really don't care about running real close to.

Foyt won't cut you off and run you down the infield or run you into a fence. I've never seen him drive dirty. He always drives a clean race. He drives hard. A lot of times he drives harder than what he should. And that's why they call him wild. But that's just his way of driving. And if a guy wants to run that hard, that's his business.

I was running the midgets and later on a few sprint cars. And then I had to go in the army. The Korean War. I never got to Korea. I never got out of the States. I spent most of my time in Georgia and Pennsylvania. In the U.S. Army, antiaircraft. From 1950 to 1952.

Toward the end I was stationed at Fort Sill in Oklahoma. That's when I started racing stock cars. I was working in the hospital at Fort Sill. I'd injured myself playing baseball. Chipped a bone in my knee. And when I recuperated, a doctor there got me to stay on working for him. It was just a matter of about three months before I was going to be discharged. Hospital work was eight to four. That was regular duty. At night I'd slip out and go racing stock cars.

When I got out of the army, I went back to racing midgets again. In fact I went back to the East, around Indianapolis. But at that time the midgets had slowed down. The circuit was running one, two nights a week. There's no way that you could make a living up there.

I run midgets for about two months. And even though I was leading the point standings, I still wasn't making a living. So I came back to Texas and raced stock cars and sprint cars around here. That was about 1954, 1955.

But it was still pretty slow. So during the winter months I was working. I worked in the oil fields and in construction work. In the oil fields I was a roughneck. It wasn't heavy work. But it was a lot of hours. Usually you work eight hours, and then you spend another two or three hours driving back and forth. 'Cause most of the rigs are out of town somewhere.

Later came construction work. I was putting up metal ceilings and plastering over it. In '54 I got married. At that point I couldn't run around the various circuits quite as much. After about three years, though, I was getting really restless, wanting to go back to racing. So in '57 my wife and I took off for Florida. That was when they had the Tangerine Tournament. They had midget races about four nights a week. It was an invitational deal.

It was a circuit for midget racing. Miami, Orlando, Jacksonville—all over Florida. That's where I really got acquainted with Foyt. He was down there with his wife. And we spent about three months in Florida racing. We traveled some together. At times I might have two or three bad nights. If he had money, I'd get it. And other times,

I'd loan him money. It was just back and forth. Whoever was hot would be the banker.

The thing back then was that I wanted to race full time. I wasn't sure, though, that it was going to work out. I was figuring I'd have to do construction to keep going. But I got lucky and found an owner who had six midget cars. I took care of them and raced them. And when he got interested in sporty cars, I took care of them too. I did that for a couple of years. In '59 USAC started sports-car racing. When they did, I raced sports cars. Later on my owner bought a championship race car, and I drove that.

In 1960 is when I got a chance to go to Indianapolis.

I was born January 12, 1928.

It makes me the Old Man among the guys that drive at Indy. In fact, a lot of the ones around now—I ran with their daddies. Guys like Vukovich, Parsons, and Bettenhausen.

When I first came to Indy, they were just little kids running around the pits and everything. Now they're up there competing against me.

Foyt and I joke about it all the time. Every time we see one of the sons of the former drivers come up, we always say we're getting older, we might as well quit. And of course, we always come out in March.

When I was racing midgets there in the late 1940s, AAA was running Indianapolis and the big cars. Indy was no big deal to me then. I was, like I said, making anywhere from a thousand to fifteen hundred dollars a week. I figured I was doing better than most Indy drivers.

But by '60 I was interested. Tony Bettenhausen is the one who helped me find a ride with J. C. Agajanian. That year, my first time out, I finished seventh. [Ruby's Agajanian Special averaged 135.983 miles per hour.] I thought I had a third place, but I ran out of fuel late in the race.

I've run Indy every year since. The best I've done was third place in 1964. A lotta times I've been among the top ten finishers, but I never yet have managed to win the

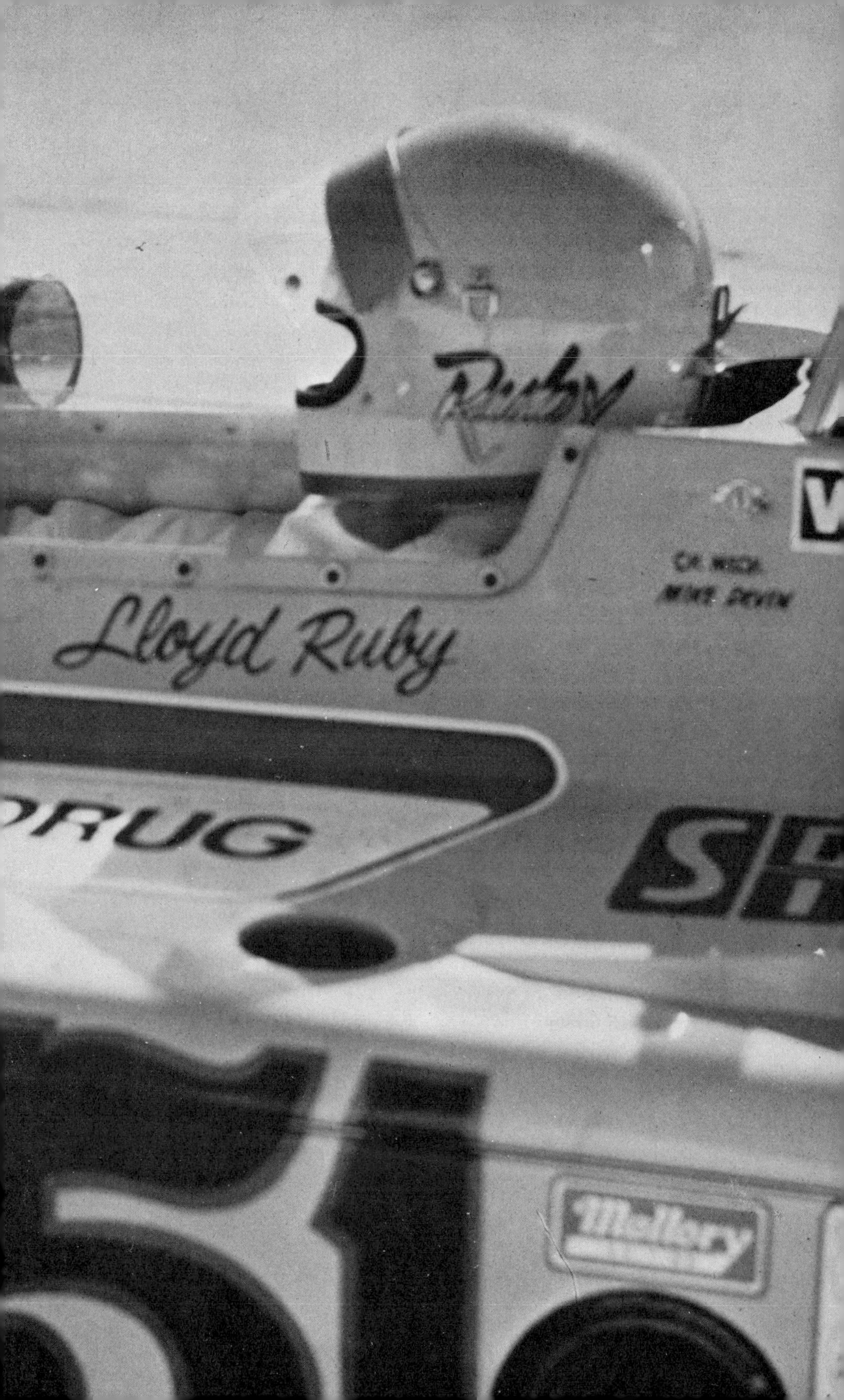
Ruby
Lloyd Ruby
DRUG

thing. Some people say I've had hard luck. But you won't hear me complain. I've taken home more than two hundred thousand dollars worth of prize money from Indy. What's more, I've had a helluva good time doing it.

Of course, I wish I could win the 500. But win or not, it's a thrill to keep coming back. I said I was going to quit five, six years ago. But it's just hard to get out of it.

After the first of the year, I find I'm thinking about Indy. I visualize the track and the things that have happened there that took me out of races. And I kind of visualize what I hope's going to happen that year. I know something's gonna break, but each year I gotta go back and see what it is. [Laughs.]

With me, there's plenty to think about as far as Indy is concerned. Like 1966. That year I was leading the field. There were only fifty laps left. I got flagged off the track on account of an oil leak. Do you know that I led the race more laps than any other driver?

It was worse in 1968. I was out ahead of the pack with only twenty-five laps to go. And what happens? The coil broke. It cost me six minutes in the pits. By the time I came back on to the track, I was out of it. I finished fifth that year.

Nineteen sixty-nine, I couldn't blame it on luck. That year I messed up. I'd come into the pits for fuel. And before the crew could disconnect the last fueling hose, I gave it the gas. It tore the tank right off the car.

I've seen Indy change over the years. In my opinion, it's changed for the better. I remember, though, the first time they brought rear-end cars to Indy. I figured one of those cars hit the wall, you could just take a blotter and wipe the driver off the wall. I mean, that's the way it looked.

But actually they're a lot safer than the roadsters were. 'Cause when they do hit the wall, you'll see the wheels knock off. What it does as it breaks off, it absorbs part of the blow. Then your wheels are off of it, and it'll just slide. I've had two or three pretty good crashes. And I believe if it had been a roadster, I wouldn't have survived.

Of course, my attitude toward racing has changed.

That's natural, though. When I was a kid, it was an adventure. Shoot, in the midgets, you could get upside down or through the fence once every two weeks or so, but you didn't think a thing about it. Later on you might still get in trouble, but you looked at it in a more businesslike way.

I may be old. But I'm still fit to drive. I work at it. Off-seasons I work with the weights. The little cars, rear-engine cars, are much easier to drive than big roadsters or dirt cars were. Most of it is in your arms.

I'll work with the weights in my house. Lying there watching television, I'll push them during commercials. I've got barbells and dumbbells both. I keep one hundred pounds on the barbell and just keep cranking 'em out.

When I'm in my passenger car, there are handgrips. I just automatically pick them up every time I get in the car. It helps your grip. While I'm driving with one hand, I'll be squeezing the grip with the other. Just keep changing hands.

Like I say, I'm in shape. You ask some of the younger drivers. I'm always arm wrestling a lot of what I call the young kids. The ones who think they're strong. None of the drivers has put me down. I don't know about Foyt. I never have played with him. Gary Bettenhausen kept saying there's some trick to it. But it's no trick. It's just pure strength.

I'm still driving Indy because I want to. I could get out anytime. I've invested in some oil royalties, and I'm a partner in a steel company. With what I've got saved up I could quit and no problem.

But I keep coming back because it's in my blood. I'm a driver.

wally dallenbach

WALLY DALLENBACH runs the Wood'n Handle Ranch
in Colorado. But that's for the future.
For now he runs Indy cars.

Since 1973 I've run a one-hundred-and-sixty-acre guest ranch up here in the Rocky Mountains called the Wood'n Handle Ranch. It's located in Frying Pan Valley. You can't find anything more western than those names.

There were nine cabins on the property when I bought the ranch. I've added five more since then. When I'm through racing, I'll be at the ranch full time with my wife, Peppy, and our three kids. It's my security for the future.

For most of my career in racing driving's been more of a sport than a profession. In the last few years things have been coming together for me in racing—ever since 1973, actually, when I hooked up with the Patrick Racing Team and mechanic George Bignotti.

But even if my racing hadn't gotten to the point where it is now—where I am guaranteed good equipment for every race—I would have combined racing with other business interests. Back in East Brunswick, New Jersey, before we moved out to the mountains, I had a Goodyear tire store and I was a part owner of a pipeline construction company with my cousin, Richie Massing.

Richie and I used to race stock cars together. We ran numbers 35A and 35B. He knew racing, and he always understood why I had to be away from the business for long periods of time. We got along real well together. When we moved to Colorado, he bought me out, and now he owns the construction company all by himself.

I always spent a lot of time in Colorado, and I always felt I'd end up living in the mountains. I went to high school in Westminster, near Denver, because I lived with my brother for a few years out there. His name is Robert, and he's a minister in the Pillar of Fire Church which has about five thousand worshippers around the country, many of them in the Denver area. It's a fundamentalist kind of Methodism. Stricter than regular Methodism. I went to Pillar of Fire School in Westminster those years I was living with my brother. This gave me the opportunity to spend a lot of time in the Rockies, which led to my eventual move to my ranch and a more basic down-to-earth way of life.

I came to regard New Jersey as just a place to live and the place where I was from. Even when we lived there, we'd go off into the mountains in Vermont and Pennsylvania for weekends to ski and ride bikes and snowmobiles. So finally we said, "Instead of just going to the mountains on weekends, why don't we just live there?" The Colorado mountains appealed to us more than the eastern ones, so we just came out. I do miss a lot of my eastern friends, though. But now they have an excuse to come out and visit me.

I always loved cars and machinery. I guess I got that from my late father. He owned a sand and gravel company in East Brunswick and used to like to make all his own repairs on cars and things with the machinery he owned. My brother and two sisters never were too interested in that stuff, but I was. And I was the baby of the family—I was born December 12, 1936—so maybe I got away with more than the others.

By the time I was fifteen, I was building cars. See, I already had my sights set on racing. I'd come back to New Jersey during the summers after I finished a year of school in Colorado. There were very few opportunities in Colorado for kids interested in cars, so in the summers was when I'd fool around with cars.

When I was fourteen, I bought myself an old 1935 Ford coupé. It cost me thirty-five dollars—a dollar a year. I cut it down, painted it, and put roll bars on it. I was always mechanically inclined. As far back as I can remember, I was good with cars and engines and bikes and all that kind of stuff.

I was too young to get a driver's license, so I'd drive the car around the back roads of my father's sand and gravel company. Every now and then I'd sneak out and run on the regular roads with it.

When I turned seventeen and got my driver's license, I went into drag racing. It was the only kind of racing I was allowed in. Dragging was a young sport then. Most of the guys in it were in their late teens and early twenties.

First I drove a B-gas sedan, and I worked up to the fastest sedan class, A-gas. I was in it five years, and all that time I tried being an individualist. I've always been like that. Everybody in dragging was running Chryslers, so I ran a Buick. Everybody ran slingshot racers, those long, low jobs with the engine in the front; I built a rear-engine machine. Today that's common, but in those days it was pretty unique.

I ran in the major national dragging events, the Winternationals in Daytona, Florida, and in Charlotte, North Carolina and all over. And we did pretty well. I wasn't always top dog, but I won my share of big races.

As soon as I turned twenty-one, I got out of dragging. I always knew I would. I just stuck with drag racing until I was old enough to get into oval racing. There was a lot of local small-time racing in New Jersey, New York, and Pennsylvania, so I raced all over in those states. I knew this was what I liked best, and my parents, who had been pretty apprehensive about my racing up to that time, began to realize if racing was something I wanted to do, then I must do it.

I put my dragster engine into a stock car and had pretty good success with it for a couple years. One year at Wall Stadium in Vineland, New Jersey, I won fourteen out of twenty-two events. That was 1962.

In 1963 I built up a new stock car, but my heart wasn't really in it. What I actually wanted was a ride in an open-wheel car. I was always talking to owners of midgets, but nothing was coming of it.

Then one day at a race I talked with Nick Dueno from New Brunswick, who owned a midget. His son had been killed in the car, and there was a lot of sentiment attached to it. He seemed willing to consider the idea of giving me a test drive, so I went out to race my stock car figuring his eyes would be on me.

Well, I won my heat, and then I was on my way to winning the feature event when another car got crossed up in front of me. Over the wall I went, end over end. My brand new car. "Well," I thought, "there goes me with Dueno." But a few days later he called me up. We took the midget down to the track on an off-night and played around with it. It ended up that I drove for him the rest of that year, and all of the next.

It was a turning point for me. I really loved that open cockpit racing! Once I got in that car I said to myself, "This is the place where I want to be." I knew I absolutely had to go on. I knew I was going to Indy.

Of course, you don't go from a midget racer to a championship car overnight. You need a name and you need experience, and I didn't have either at that time. I drove as much as I could; midgets, sprints—stock cars, too. When I finally felt I was ready, I went around to the championship events and started talking to people. A fellow named Mel Nelson owned a roadster, and one day his driver didn't show up. I said to him, "Look, let me drive it in the next race. I'll guarantee you I'll qualify it in the starting field, and I'll guarantee you I'll finish the race. And if I crash it, I'll fix it at my expense."

Well, he thought about it and finally he called me up and said okay. The next race was at Langhorne, Pennsylvania, one of the regular stops on the Championship Trail of USAC racing. My first ride in a championship car— that was in 1965. It wasn't much of an experience. We had a leak in the cockpit that practically fried me in hot oil. I got blisters on my face and neck and hands. There was only a half-gallon left in the tank at the end of the race. We were not black flagged—told to stop—because the car was black. The stewards couldn't see the oil on the car, although I was soaking most of it up myself. It was so bad I drove the last seventy-five laps without goggles.

It was my own stupid determination not to give up. I'd made all those guarantees to Mel Nelson, see?

Wally Dallenbach

124

When you get into big-league racing, it's very hard to establish a good ride. All the cars look new and shiny, but there's a big difference between them. When you drive with professional, high-priced equipment, you have to work your way through different levels of equipment and hope to get a better ride each year. It was very difficult, my first four or five years in championship racing, to get a first-class ride.

But I kept at it, and I went to Indy the first time in 1967 in a car that couldn't do much. I went seventy-three laps before having a minor accident and we were credited with twenty-ninth place in the final standings.

I was already past thirty years old, but with my other businesses—the pipeline construction outfit and other things—I was moving up in racing on my own timetable. Very few guys can come into championship racing in their twenties and have any success, because no matter how good a driver is, he still has to work his way into good equipment. Car owners don't just let anybody have a good ride, you know.

Besides that, I'm not in favor of just letting a guy talk himself into a ride. I'm a believer in letting water seek its own level. If a guy has the determination he's got to have, he'll make it on his own.

There's more to it nowadays, though, than just learning how to drive a race car. That was true in the old days, but it isn't anymore. None of that, "I'm gonna drive the wheels off this S.O.B." Nowadays plain old talent is only a percentage of it. The rest is politics. See, you're going to be talking to millionaires. Men with a high degree of intelligence, mental toughness, business sense. You've got to be able to put yourself over to them. Some kids haven't learned to sell themselves well. You won't necessarily talk yourself into a ride—I really don't believe you can—but you've got to show a certain toughness and sense of yourself. If you don't leave an owner with a good impression of yourself today, chances are you won't get a look from that same owner somewhere down the road when you're ready for his equipment.

My big problem at Indy over the years has been mechanical attrition. In fact, I've had that same problem in a lot of my races in general. That's my big regret—not winning more races, races I should have won because I was in good cars. I think I could have won twenty more championship car races than I have if my equipment had held up. In ninety percent of the races I didn't finish, there was some kind of mechanical failure.

I should have won the 1975 Indianapolis race. I came within eight minutes of winning that. And I should have won the 1974 Pocono 500. I came within six minutes of winning that. The engine burned out both times.

The biggest disappointment was the 1975 Indianapolis race. I had a twenty-four-second lead when I had to come out. Twelve laps later it rained, and when it got real bad, they had to call off the race with only one hundred and seventy-four of the two hundred laps completed. Bobby Unser got the win. If I still had been running in the lead when the rains came, naturally I would have been the winner. Instead I got only ninth place for completing one hundred and sixty-two laps.

Another disappointment was the 1974 Indianapolis race. I qualified for the middle of the first row with a speed up in the 190s. But I lasted only three laps in the race itself when a piston broke. That was one year when we all felt —George Bignotti and our whole crew and Pat Patrick, our owner—that we had a real shot at winning the race. We ran the fastest competitive lap that's ever been run at Indy, more than 191 miles per hour. It's in the *Guinness Book of World Records*. But it didn't do us any good when we lasted only three laps altogether.

The biggest win I've ever had was in the 1973 Ontario 500. In that one, everything came together just right. The racing luck stayed with us all day.

Nineteen seventy-three was the year when they had

a real bad Indianapolis 500. Drivers were getting killed and injured all over the place, and USAC took measures to cut down on the speeds by limiting the fuel you could have in your tank, reducing the amount of boost you could have in your turbocharger, and some other things.

We went through a year and a half of going through different fuel mixtures and different valves. In order to win and lead races, we had to mix fuels many different ways. We could have played it safe and been satisfied to go after fifth and sixth places. But we were out to win. The fact we didn't win more than we did was just one of those things that happen.

It might sound strange, when we're talking about cars going 190, 195 miles an hour at Indianapolis, 'but I've always been very safety conscious about racing. It's not necessary to go these speeds to please the fans. Three hundred thousand people will still come to the Speedway every May to see the race whether we're going 180 or 200 miles an hour. I say 180 to 190 because that's a safe speed for us. 195 to 200-plus miles an hour is a very dangerous speed for us. If you're going that fast, that you can't negotiate a turn it's not the driver anymore who's in control. You climb up to a tremendous average speed, and you reduce the amount of reaction time you have in the turns. That's where the problems exist—in those corners. The straightaways are fine; we can go 195 to 220 miles an hour on the straights, and we're okay. A guy going from the fuel dragsters they run today, which can go about 250 miles an hour, would get into an Indy racer and have a hell of a time adjusting. He'd be going so much slower down a straightaway. But the turns are where you're going to have trouble.

This is why I get mad when people say auto racing isn't a sport. Auto racing is more demanding than most other sports. There's the concentration factor. I don't care what sport you pick out. You concentrate for a few minutes, an inning, a round, whatever it is. We have to concentrate totally for hours sometimes. We're traveling three hundred feet a second. If you forget yourself for a second, you're three hundred feet in the wall.

One thing about our sport, too, is the amazing competition. Even with the rules that USAC has put in to reduce fuel and all that, people keep finding new ways to go faster and faster. There are better and wider tires, better suspension systems, better everything. As fast as the new rules come in, racing teams manage to find a way to still go faster. That's the nature of the competition in racing. I'm not so sure it's good to keep going faster and faster, but how're you going to stop it?

And being the kind of people we are in this sport, we keep running in races no matter what the speeds are. We do amazing things in the heat of competition. After I had that experience at Langhorne, when I got soaked in hot oil back in 1965, I told myself I'd never do that again. But a couple of years later at Phoenix I got some burns on my heels. A panel came loose and let hot radiator air in. But I didn't stop. Those burns took five months to heal. I ran Indy that year in tennis shoes, two sizes too large and wadded with bandages.

Then there was another day at Milwaukee that was extremely hot and humid. A lot of guys dropped out with heat exhaustion. The steering wheel was so hot in my hands I couldn't move them to a new place. But I wouldn't quit because I was leading. I led two-thirds of that race.

Like I say, it's amazing what you'll go through in the heat of competition. The strain of driving is more than enough, and if you have to fight the car if it's handling badly or something, it really wears you out. A lot of times you just hang in there waiting for that second wind. But sometimes it never comes, and then you're just worn out.

I once had a problem in a champ car race car at Dover, Delaware. This was 1969. The track at Dover had very high banking. I never liked that kind of track. But anyway, the suspension gave out and I hit the wall. Then the car caught fire. I tried to get out, but the chassis had crushed around my ankles. I couldn't pull my left foot out.

It was getting pretty hot. The rubber on the steering

wheel was melting down into my lap. You can believe I wanted to get out of there. So I actually tried to pull my foot off. Finally it came out, and the only damage was three broken toes.

This safety thing is very serious business with me. You know we go fast at Indianapolis, but they've had years and years of experience. But at some of the newer tracks, where you're going faster even than at Indianapolis, how much experience do the crews have?

I was down testing at Texas International Speedway a few years back, and I really felt I was in five times as much danger down there. I asked the fire crew to gather around the car while I showed them a few things. Like how to pull me out. First the steering wheel must be turned so the cut-out sector is at the bottom or I can't get out. Then I have to be pulled out backward, not straight up, or else my legs will jam the instrument panel. They didn't know about any of that. They were willing, but they were just a bunch of college boys. They didn't have any experience at this type of thing.

With all that goes into racing and the expenses involved in getting a car on the track at Indianapolis and the other major races, I have to laugh sometimes when people think we get a lot of money. The winning car at Indianapolis gets about two hundred thousand dollars or so. But, of course, the driver doesn't get all of that. The owner gets a piece, but it's rarely enough to cover his expenses at putting the racing team together. Usually, the car owner hopes he can get a sponsor or two to cover some of the expense. But the sponsors get a share of any money the car wins.

But when you start looking at what some golfers and tennis pros are getting, and the kind of contracts some of the basketball and baseball and football players have, I would say we're grossly underpaid. In the other sports they have year-to-year contracts. Compare that to our situation. We start each year with no guarantee of anything. We start all over each year. And when you consider the risks we take to make our money, there's no comparison with other sports. Besides all that, you can't take this sport in college or high school or anywhere else. You've got to do this on your own.

It's an exception in this sport to have the kind of family life I have. The atmosphere in racing is very tempting, especially at the highest levels. You're always vulnerable. You're in the public eye, and you have to mind your P's and Q's. You have to tell yourself your wife and your kids come first, or else it can wreck your marriage. But a lot of the guys don't bother about it.

With us, racing has always been a family thing. Our three kids, Wally Junior, Colleen, and Paul, all know racing very well, and they enjoy it. Wally, who's thirteen now, wants to go racing when he gets older. I'll let him seek his own level. He's very agile. He's very good on a bike and on a snowmobile, so he's got the physical qualifications.

All three kids love it in Colorado. They have horses, snowmobiles, mini-bikes, all this land and their freedom. What kid wouldn't like it?

My wife, Peppy—her real name's Annette—is real great about it, too. It was a traumatic thing for us to make this big a move. Peppy's Italian, so her family is very close-knit, and it was tough for her to break away. But she loves skiing, and she's great at it too, so she's made a whole new circle of friends here in the mountains. Overall, the move has turned out great for us.

The big inconvenience is in traveling to the races. You can't get anywhere from here without first flying into Denver and then going from there to wherever the race is. We're about twenty miles from the airport in Aspen, so we catch a flight from there down to Denver.

Peppy's relatives like to ski, too, so they come out to see us pretty often. So we manage to stay in pretty good contact with most of them.

Up where we live, it's kind of tough to earn a living unless you're very humble and are willing to do anything just to be able to live in the mountains, or very versatile and do lots of different things. It's mostly young singles or couples up here. They come for the skiing or the certain kind of life they like in the mountains, and they might stay for the six-month winter season or the six-month summer season. If a guy comes up here with a trade, he's fortunate if he gets to work that trade. Most likely, he'll end up washing dishes or hustling around doing as many different things as possible. If it was easy to live up here, everybody would be here.

Like I said, this ranch we have up here is our security for the future. Many drivers now have good investments, or they know people who invest their money for them. But a few guys just squander their money away, and when they can't race anymore, they don't have anything. I made up my mind a long time ago that this wasn't going to happen to me. Eventually, we'll have more cabins that we'll be able to rent at our ranch, and we should be able to make a real good living out of it.

One of the things I'm real proud of is my gun collection. I'm a very avid hunter, and for about twenty-five years, since I was a teen-ager, I've collected guns. I have about thirty-five now, and two of them, Colt pistols about ninety years old, are worth about five thousand dollars each. I usually try to buy two or three guns a year. I'll go around looking for them, or I'll hear from someone who has a gun to sell. I also have some friends always looking for guns I might be interested in buying. I have some guns I use for hunting, but I also have some I'll never fire. Those I keep just for display.

It'll be tough to leave racing. Not so much for the money, which is pretty good, but because I've been in it for a long time, and it's hard to give up something you like. I'm a little worried about where the sport is going, though. The higher speeds of the cars indicate progress. But you have to marry progress with common sense. It's common sense that when you start hurting drivers, you have to do something about it. At Indianapolis they've repaved the track and made the walls higher, but who knows if all that is going to help?

Still, I'll keep at it for a while yet because it's my sport. I still think I can accomplish a few things in it yet. This is one sport where experience counts a lot, so even at forty I'm able to keep on improving, whereas in other sports I'd be considered washed up.

It's more comfortable for me to race now than it has been ever. Because of my experience and common-sense knowledge I feel more at home in a race car than I did five years ago.

mark donohue

MARK DONOHUE thought he'd had enough of
auto racing, and retired. He could not resist
coming back, though.

My father, Mark Senior, a graduate of Harvard Law School, is a partner in a New York City law firm that specializes in patent law. He always wanted my two sisters and me to get a college education. I did—at Brown University in Providence, Rhode Island, where I got a Bachelor of Science degree in mechanical engineering.

The fact that I went to college makes me unusual in racing circles. There are drivers who never even finished high school. But a college degree doesn't mean a thing in this sport. People think I have some sort of "unfair advantage" because I know more about the mechanical side of racing than other drivers. That's nonsense. Racing is a business like everything else. To be successful in it, you just have to put in the time. That's what we've done. And if that's unfair, fine. Let people call it unfair.

To be racing in this kind of competition, every driver has to have what we call a "seat-of-the-pants" feeling about the car. If you don't know enough to pull into the pits and have the car looked at when you think there may be a problem, you don't belong on the track in the first place. Of course my mechanical knowledge helps. Sometimes I'm able to tell my crew where to look right away so they can fix a problem very quickly. But, hell, all my education doesn't help me a bit when I'm out there in the corners, trying to go faster.

Even as a kid in Summit, New Jersey, I knew that I would end up driving race cars. I went to college and then worked in the construction business. But they were just things to do while I got settled in racing. You could say I got my "start" in racing when I was nine, in our driveway. It was awkward and tricky to back a car out of it. It took a lot of "backing and forthing" to get it parked in the barn, which was our garage, facing forward. But I kept working at it until I mastered it. Then I just kept on doing it at increasing speeds. I never had an accident, though I ruined some flower beds a few times.

My father would say, "Mark, don't fool around like that with the car and stop taking chances."

I would say, "When I'm doing something, I don't fool around. I try to do it right and not take any chances."

Most drivers have a high threshold of pain. Aches and bruises in this business you just shrug off. I remember in the spring of 1971 practicing for a race in Langhorne, Pennsylvania, when a piece of metal that was on the track flew up and caught me in the eye. They rushed me to the hospital, and the doctors barely saved it. Then they bandaged me up. A few days later I made a promotional appearance in New York still wearing the bandage.

People came up to me after and asked me how I could talk about going racing so soon after that kind of injury. I said, "Hey, this is my business. Nobody's forcing me to do this. I like it, so I accept any problems that may come up from time to time."

Long before that, I was very accustomed to pain. By the time I was seven, I had already had scarlet fever, a tonsillectomy, vein cauterizations, and a mild case of polio. I contracted polio in November 1944, when I was seven, and I was fine by the following spring. Fortunately, nothing on my body was withered, but my legs were pretty weak for a long time after that.

Two weeks after I first got polio I had spasms, the kind that cripples you. At that time hospitals were afraid to keep polio victims around because they didn't know how the contagion was spread. This was about ten years before the Salk vaccine. There was something called the Sister Kenny treatment for polio. My parents tore up an old red blanket, soaked the strips in boiling water, and wrapped them around my legs—this was how the treatment worked —to prevent the muscles from atrophying while I was having these spasms.

I came through okay. People remarked later how amazing it was that through all the sickness and treatments I never cried. Or hardly ever, anyway. They wondered how did I keep from crying. Well, I told them, you just say to yourself you won't, and you don't. You just clamp your teeth. That's what I always tell myself when something happens to me in racing too.

I suppose we race drivers all are a little strange in some ways. We certainly have a lot less fear of the unknown than most other people. Sometimes this leads us to do some weird things. I did something when I was about twelve that I wouldn't admit was weird at the time but, now that I'm looking back on it, really was.

I was fooling around with an old Ford in the barn, and the barn caught fire. My mother and two sisters, Nancy and Emmie, were in the kitchen. I ran toward the house, screaming for them to call the fire department. Then I ran back into the fire. See, the fire had started under the car, and I knew where the fire extinguisher was. So after I ran toward the house, I ran back to the barn, grabbed the fire extinguisher off the wall, shot it at all the likely places, and put the fire out before the fire department guys got there.

My mother was angry. She said there was no reason to have taken such a risk. I told her then, and my father when he got back home that night, that it had been a calculated risk, that I had known just what I was doing. I have to admit, though, that maybe I wouldn't do that again now. Risk taking, unnecessary risk taking, just isn't me. I don't gamble crazily. In a race car, people think you're always gambling, taking risks. But I don't look at it that way. If you know what you're doing, it's not as big a gamble as all that.

I always make it a point to try to find out as much as I can about anything I do. That's the way it's always been for me with racing. I fooled around with racing on some small local tracks in New England when I was at Brown. But before I did it, I talked about it with guys who had some experience, and I checked things out carefully. In school, and then back home during the summers, I fell in with fellows who liked racing. We all tried our hand at it, to the point of driving south all night to Florida for small sports-car races and then turning around and coming right back north after the races.

I started out in a small car, and right away I was winning. I had about forty races my first year and won maybe ninety percent of them. My first competitive race was a hill climb in my Corvette back in 1960. A guy named Burge Hulett and I just decided one Tuesday afternoon we wanted to race. On Wednesday we went to a Sports Car Club of America (SCCA) regional dinner as guests, and the following Saturday, we were racing up the hill.

My first driver's school was at Marlboro, a real twister of a circuit in Massachusetts. My instructor was an AC Bristol driver, Pierre Mion. Pierre drove my Elva Courier for ten laps, got out, and said "go ahead," and I never saw him again. Not that day, anyway. But that was all the instruction I ever did get from him.

I qualified for my SCCA license that weekend, which was par for the course in those days, and two weeks later I entered a regional race in Lime Rock, Connecticut, where I finished fourth with my Elva. More important to me than the fourth place was the knowledge that what the car lacked were those certain bits and pieces that would turn a street car into a racing machine.

So I went over and had a talk with my mechanic, Lou Schultz, and he gave me a list of what he figured we needed. I then coughed up seven hundred dollars, and Lou bought and attached what I needed, and I headed for Vineland, New Jersey, where I won fifteen straight races.

In my first national race at Lime Rock, Charlie Kolb, who had a pretty fair reputation in the area, was considered the favorite, but my Courier ran beautifully and I managed to beat Charlie to the checkered flag.

Then 1961 was a whirlwind year. We traveled to races all over the country, from Daytona to Watkins Glen, Marlboro, Cumberland—even a race in an airport at Montgomery, Alabama. There were three of us who fought for the title in our class of cars—me, Peter Revson in a Morgan, and Jay Signore, also in an Elva. I managed to come out on top.

This still was far from the big leagues of racing, and I wasn't making any money at all from it. I was working as a technical consultant for a pulverizing company just to keep out of hock. I didn't really know what was going to happen with my racing, and after the chassis broke on my car at Sebring early in 1962, I had to stop. I was broke and couldn't afford to spend anymore money to keep racing.

For the entire summer of '62 I did nothing—not in racing, that is. I did write a letter to Elva Cars in England to tell them what a shame it was that the chassis on my car broke. In July I got a pleasant surprise. Elva sent me a new chassis free of charge. Between July and December I changed the chassis and rebuilt the engine, and I was back in business.

It was at this time I started to learn as much as I could about the cars I was driving. I couldn't even adjust the valves on my first Elva. Now, though, that there was no money to pay other people for maintaining the car, I learned how to take care of it. I learned how to change the brakes, gearboxes, clutches, rear ends—you name it. I looked at what other people were doing and tried to do better. And I kept on winning races, which made everything nice.

It wasn't the only nice thing that happened. By '63 I'd met my wife, Sue. We married a few months after her sister introduced us.

By the '70s, the marriage was a washout. Sue came to resent the many hours I was putting in with Roger Penske in our all-round racing program. Sometimes I would sleep on a cot in the garage to get an early start the next morning, and Sue would get angry.

But hooking up with Roger changed my career. We put together one of the best all-round programs anyone ever has, a program that produced top cars for just about every major form of racing there is—Indy racing, stock-car racing, Formula One racing, sports-car racing, you name it.

When I first met Roger, he suggested I test-drive a car for him that would be driven by someone else. He liked what I did so much, pretty soon I was his regular driver.

Some people call me a perfectionist, and maybe I am. My father once said, "If you take care of all the little things, the big things will take care of themselves." It's a philosophy that's worked for me, especially in racing.

Like me, Roger has never been able to settle for anything less than a first-class effort. He could have been one of the top professional racedrivers himself—he was a great amateur sports-car racer. But he decided to concentrate on business. Penske Enterprises at Penske Plaza in Reading, Pennsylvania, is a sure sign that he's succeeded.

Roger is probably best known for having a wrecked race car rebuilt overnight. Even people in racing can't believe how much drive he has and how he can instill this drive in so many people. His capacity for coping with an unforeseen or unusual challenge is extraordinary.

With Roger to back me, I was finally able to get into professional racing full time. At that time they had a professional series of sports-car races called the U.S. Road Racing Championships. In 1967 and 1968 I won that championship driving for Penske. Then, when that series was discontinued in 1969, I concentrated on winning the Trans-American Sedan Series in a specially prepared Chevrolet Camaro.

I also participated in the Canadian-American Challenge Series for Unlimited Sports Cars, generally called Can-Am racing, and had a run of pretty high finishes for a few years, driving a Penske-Lola.

I can't remember when Roger and I first started talking about going to Indianapolis. Indy never was a particularly big dream of mine. I liked sports cars and Formula cars and road racing. I didn't know much at all about oval racing and didn't particularly care to know that much about it. To me, it represented a different world of people, different cars, an entirely different setup.

But then Roger started talking with me about Indy and the Speedway. He felt that no matter how many races we won in Can-Am or Trans-Am or anything, the kind of racing most people care about in this country is oval racing. Stocks and Indy-type cars. "The Indy 500 is the biggest thing in this sport in the United States," Roger said. And he was right. In Europe, people don't much care who wins Indy, but in this country racing fans don't much care who wins the Belgian Grand Prix or the British Grand Prix. It became obvious to me that we had to take a shot at Indy.

When we went to Indy at the beginning of May in 1969, there were certain drivers there who wanted us to fail. Racing is funny that way. If you've been successful in one form of racing, many guys in another type of racing resent it when you try their game. They think you're trying to tell them, "Okay, boys, move over, the new man is here."

It's not like that at all. At least, it wasn't for me and Roger. We had a tremendous respect for the drivers at the Speedway and what they were doing. I knew there was no way we were going to come in as newcomers and dominate this bunch.

But there were strange vibes going around; I could feel it. I was considered different from the other Indy drivers. I had grown up in the East, I had gone to college, I was articulate, I didn't swear a lot—and I looked so damn young. I've always looked younger than I was, and even though I was thirty-two years old when I first showed up at the Speedway, I probably looked like I was twenty-five or so.

Another thing too: I picked up a nickname in sports-car racing, the kind of nickname that turned off a lot of the Indy drivers—Captain Nice. This had nothing to do with my racing style. On the track I'm as competitive as

can be. Rather it had to do with my quiet way of going
about things. My quiet way of talking to people, and so
on. In a way it was like the opposite of A. J. Foyt's nickname, Tough Tony. (His real first name is Anthony.) He
was generally considered tough to deal with, tough to
know, tough to talk to. I was sort of easygoing and all
that, so I was Captain Nice.

But that wasn't entirely accurate either. It's true that
I'm usually agreeable. But if it's a couple of days before a
big race like the Indianapolis 500 and someone comes up
to me and asks me something not directly connected with
the race or wants to make small talk, he's going to walk
away thinking I'm pretty awful. I'm not in a mood for
small talk then.

So, anyway, we went to the Speedway in 1969, and I
passed my rookie test. In the qualifying trials for the race
I was fourth fastest.

That was also Peter Revson's first year at Indy. We
knew each other from road racing. He also wasn't certain
whether he liked Indy as much as road racing, but he'd
been persuaded to try it. Peter barely made the field,
qualifying for the thirty-third and last spot.

We didn't think we had a chance to win, even though
our fourth qualifying spot was better than we had expected coming in. Not long after the race started, my car
started having troubles. There was something wrong with
the fuel mix, and the car was malfunctioning. We never
did quite get it all worked out, and I had to drive like hell
a few times just to keep the car from going into the wall.
We ended up in seventh place, pretty good under the circumstances.

I was voted the top rookie in the race, but a lot of people
figured that Revson should have gotten it. He finished fifth
in the race after starting thirty-third, and that's pretty rare.
Starting that far back, your chances of finishing up among
the leaders are remote. So a lot of people thought that
Peter should have gotten top rookie. One of those people
was Peter. He was pretty cool toward me for a while after

that. It wasn't my fault. I didn't have a vote. I don't know why the voting turned out the way it did. But that's the way it goes.

We learned a lot from that first Indy experience and came back in 1970 thinking we had a good chance to win the whole thing. We weren't interested in running the other races on the USAC circuit, since Roger and I really were road-racing guys at heart.

But once we had our first taste of Indy we wanted to come back and win there. We had a pretty good car in 1970. It qualified fifth. But that was the year Al Unser won Indy from the pole position, leading nearly the entire race. I finished second, but wasn't close. I probably should have been satisfied with that. I wasn't. Back to the drawing board.

Nineteen seventy-one was going to be our year at Indianapolis. We thought we came in with the best car. On the fifth or sixth day of practice I broke the track record by going more than 177 miles per hour—8 miles faster than the old record. About a week after that I ran 180 miles an hour. Everyone was going wild.

We forgot one thing, though. Speed isn't the primary goal in racing. What good is it to have the fastest car if it only lasts a few miles? The car has to stay together for the entire race. At Indianapolis you have to go five hundred miles in order to win.

I took the early lead in 1971, and was putting distance between myself and the other drivers for the first hundred miles or so. But I was worried it was going too easy. I was right. A gearbox snapped and I finally had to come out of the race on the sixty-sixth lap. That was a bad joke. I always have driven the number-66 car, which is kind of a lucky number for Roger and me, but this time the number 66 was our bad luck lap.

Up until that time the Indy 500 was the longest USAC race. So you couldn't get any long-distance experience in a USAC car anywhere else. But in 1971 they had the first Schaefer 500 at Pocono Raceway. We won it starting from the pole. We knew what winning a long Indy-type race

Sunoco Special McLaren
WINS INDY 500

SUNOCO 66

DONOHUE
ECORDS:

felt like. That helped in getting ready for the next year's Indy race.

In 1972 we came in with an "underpowered" car. It was intentional. We wanted something that would hold up for the full distance and that would give us good, not necessarily exceptional, speeds on the straights and in the corners.

It turned out to be the right thing to do. It surprised us that we still managed to qualify for the front row, with Bobby Unser and Revson. My speed was 191-something, which gives you some idea of how fast those other guys were going.

But, like I say, the race was the main thing to us. And everything worked the way it was supposed to. It was one of the smoothest rides I ever had in my life. The car was fantastic, and we set an average speed record for the entire race. Bobby's and Peter's cars, by the way, went out early with mechanical failures. So that showed that the fastest cars for short distances weren't necessarily the best cars in the race.

At that point I first started thinking about retiring from racing, the driving part anyway. I was thirty-five years old. Roger wanted me to become full-time manager of the racing team and work on developing new cars. He also wanted me to keep on driving. I didn't think I wanted to do both. I figured I couldn't keep on driving until I was sixty-five, so maybe that was the time to just get out of driving.

But, of course, I didn't. A few weeks after I won Indy I was testing a new Porsche prototype at Road Atlanta when the steering disintegrated right on the track. I tore up my left knee pretty badly. The bottom of my leg was turned away from the knee, and I had to stay in the hospital for a few weeks until the whole thing came together again.

Even then I couldn't quit. Besides winning Indianapolis, our big ambition that year was to break Team

McLaren's monopoly on the Can-Am circuit. Ironically, McLaren had worked with us in our Indy program, and we had won in a McLaren car. But in Can-Am we had a deal with Porsche and thought we could finally stop McLaren, which had won the Can-Am series something like five or six years in a row.

But after my accident in Atlanta, I was through for most of the rest of the year, so we concentrated on getting everything together for the 1973 Can-Am. We ended up winning most of the races in that and the overall championship. We went to Indy again and didn't do much there—fifteenth place. I had to come out after ninety-two laps with a burned piston. But Roger and I were getting into more and more different things. We tried a couple of NASCAR stock races and won one, the Riverside 500 in California, driving a Matador. That made me one of the very few drivers in history ever to win in sports cars, Indy cars, and stocks.

This time, I figured, it really was time to quit. I had a big responsibility managing the racing team, working with the other drivers, and I was pretty well set up financially. So why not quit?

I might have stayed retired for good right then if the International Race of Champions hadn't been set up. They picked twelve of the top drivers from all classifications, gave each of us an identical Porsche Carrera to drive, and put us in a series of four races to see how we all came out.

That was in the early part of 1974, and I won the thing, which, next to winning Indianapolis, I guess has been my biggest victory. It was a pretty good idea having all of us run against each other—Foyt; Denis Hulme from the Grand Prix circuit; George Follmer, a great road racer; Bobby Unser—but the idea that we all were racing "identical" cars wasn't really true. Sure, every guy was running the same name and make machine out of the same factory. But there are little differences in every machine that make every one just a little different from every other. You see it in passenger cars all the time. You and your friend go to the same dealer, the same showroom, and pick out the same car. You both drive out with it. A year later he's still driving the same car, there's never been a moment's trouble with it. But you've had yours in the shop five or six times, and you're ready to blow up the place you bought the car from. You both bought the same car, right? Only not really.

Same thing in the IROC. I don't think it proved all that much, but it was nice to win, and attracted a lot of publicity for racing, good publicity. And that's very important to the sport and to the whole industry.

Anyway, I was sure I was never going to race again after I won that. Jackie Stewart had announced he was retiring a few months before that after setting every record there was to set in Grand Prix racing. And he was making that retirement stick. A lot of sponsors and team managers wanted him to reconsider, come back, and race again. But he told them all no. I admired Jackie for sticking to his guns. I was sure I also wouldn't be tempted to drive again either.

But I was wrong. There was one type of racing Roger and I always had talked about but never had the money or the opportunity for. Grand Prix, Formula One racing. Hardly any American drivers ever had done anything in Formula One. Revson and Mario Andretti had tried a few races here and there—mostly Peter—and had been fairly successful. We thought if we could put together a great car and really work that we could be competitive. So that's what we decided to do in 1975.

A lot of people think I'm crazy, and maybe I am. I don't need to race anymore. I think I've proved I'm one of the best. But it's actually much more than that. People think we do this to prove our manliness or whatever. But that's crazy. You do it because you like it. You don't ask anyone's permission, and you don't need it. You're driven to it.

There's a saying in racing that you think you're holding the wheel, but then you find out it's holding you. When I finally do quit it'll be for good, but I'll stay in it a while yet. Retiring from it was tougher for me than any race I've ever been in.

On August 17, 1975, Mark Donohue crashed during a practice session the morning of the Austrian Grand Prix. He died four days later of severe head injuries without ever regaining consciousness. He was thirty-eight.   **Mark Donohue**

147

dick simon

DICK SIMON has been a serious skier and parachutist. Past age thirty, he decided to try racing cars.

I've never been afraid to work hard for everything I want. It's been that way with me ever since I was a boy. My father, Ray Simon, never made a whole lot of money. He ran a bakery, a German bakery in Seattle, Washington. I was born there on Sept. 21, 1933. My father's parents came from Germany. He made things like pumpernickel bread and strudel and donuts with filling, but he had all sorts of other kinds of bread and cakes and pies too.

It got tough for us when my mother got multiple sclerosis. My grandmother, my mother's mother, came to live with us to take care of my mother. There really was nothing any of us—my father, my sister, my brother, and me—could do to help her except keep her comfortable. There was no cure. She just got worse and worse. There really wasn't any way of knowing how sick she was just by looking at her. She just kept wasting away inside.

She had the disease for ten years, I would say, and she would be able to do less and less the longer she had it. She'd stumble when she tried to walk, or she'd start to sit down and miss the chair. She'd be shaking or she'd run into the door. She lost her coordination and her feeling for things. Finally she died when she was just thirty-eight years old.

Naturally it was tough for my father to pay all the medical bills for my mother. But he probably could have paid them all with no problem, except for the fact that not long before my mother got sick, her brother and her father had loaned my father about five thousand dollars to buy new equipment for the bakery. So when my mother got sick, my father not only had to pay the doctor and the hospital and everything but also the loan for the equipment.

My mother's people went along with him for a period of time. But then the day came, and they went to him and said, "Ray, if you don't pay off the five grand, we'll sell off the equipment."

By this time my mother's disease really had gotten to my father. He had had it up to his ears. So he went off and started a new life for himself in Alaska on a fishing boat. When he left, my mother didn't know up from down. She died not long after that. I don't blame my father at all for leaving. He had pressure coming at him from all directions. Eventually he came back, about three or four years later, and he met a nice woman and remarried. Now he and my stepmother have a nice life for themselves in Santa Rosa, California. They manage an apartment complex, and the place provides them with an apartment of their own for nothing.

I started working for a living when I was about twelve. My mother wasn't anywhere near as sick as she eventually got, and my father, I don't think, needed money from me at that time. At least he didn't say so. But I thought that the few bucks I could bring in would help him out. But I didn't work because of that. I wanted things for myself, so I figured I would make some money and get them.

So I had several paper routes. Pretty soon I had such a big area to cover I couldn't do it on foot, so my dad and I went down to the driver's-license bureau, and he lied and told them I was sixteen—I was really only fourteen— and I got a license.

All this time I was also helping my father in the bakery, from about four-thirty in the morning to seven on schooldays and on Saturday and Sunday. I made dough and kneaded it for cookies. And I would fry donuts in big vats. I would stick them in the vats and then turn them over so they'd get done evenly. We could turn out hundreds and hundreds of those donuts in a week. They were very popular with my dad's customers.

I went to Ballard High School in Seattle, and all my

time there I also worked a couple of jobs. I never have
been the kind of person who needs a lot of sleep. Three,
maybe four hours a night is enough for me usually. I'm
glad I'm that way because there've always been so many
things I wanted to do, and I've had the energy to do 'em
without spending a lot of time sleeping.

When I was in high school, I kept working at the bakery, and after school at night I'd work in a shipyard from
three-thirty to about midnight. By this time I had quit
my paper routes. At the shipyard I would run parts to
different ships. I'd drive big trucks back and forth with
equipment, and I would stay in touch with the ships from
the trucks by radio hookups. I made real good money,
union scale, five hundred or six hundred dollars a month.

I would get home from the shipyard after midnight, do
maybe an hour's worth of studies, and get some sleep.
Even this wasn't enough action for me. I played football
for the Ballard High team. I'm not a big guy, only five-
eight, about a hundred and sixty pounds now. Then I
must have weighed about a hundred thirty-five. I wanted
to play halfback, but the coach put me in the line. One of
the big reasons was that I usually couldn't make the practice sessions because of my job at the shipyard. The half-
backs had to come to practice to learn the plays, but in
the line I could just show up for the games and still know
what to do. I was always a good athlete, which I guess
most of the drivers have to be.

I also did a lot of skiing in those days. I was basically a
ski jumper, but I also did the racing events. You know,
Alpine skiing is the slalom and the downhill, events like
that. Racing events. The ski jumping and cross-country,
those are called Nordic skiing events. I did 'em all, but
my best was ski jumping. I did that up north of Seattle.

Skiing is actually what got me into college. I got a
skiing scholarship to Wenatchee Junior College, about
a hundred and fifty miles east of Seattle. This was a good
opportunity for me, I figured, so off I went.

Under the terms of the scholarship I was supposed to
work as a headwaiter at a hotel near the school three

nights a week. But I realized right away I couldn't make enough of an income at that to live like I wanted to. I was driving a '49 convertible at that time, which was very nice for a college kid. This was around 1950 or '51, you see.

So I quit the headwaiter's job and went and got my own job with a dairy there. And I also worked at the gas station right next to the dairy. I was able to get early classes, like seven o'clock in the morning, so I'd get out of school about eleven-thirty. I'd wash up and get to the dairy at around twelve and work there until eight. Then I'd go over to the gas station and work until eleven-thirty or midnight and close it up. I always liked being around cars. Just for fun, when I was about fifteen, I took an old car of mine apart and put it together again. At the gas station I worked at in Wenatchee I pumped gas, sold tires, changed oil—all that sort of stuff. At the dairy I did some pasteurizing, some cleanup work, and I would help empty the big trucks as they would come in.

I would get home late and do some book work and then catch my usual three or four hours of sleep before I'd go to my class at seven in the morning. Because of all the hours I was working, I had the same problems with my skiing for the college that I had had with football in high school. I couldn't practice with the team during the week, but I would show up for the meets, the tournaments on the weekends, and go right ahead and compete. I still managed to do pretty well.

Skiing got me another scholarship after my two years at Wenatchee were over—a scholarship to the University of Utah in Salt Lake City. By this time my mother had died, and my father was gone. So I went down to Utah. I was always looking for different experiences, anyway, so I thought it was a good thing.

When I got to Salt Lake, again I realized that I would need some income besides the scholarship. So I went over to Hiland Dairy, which is one of the biggest in that part of the country. They had a big plant right in Salt Lake, and I went in and told them of my past experience. They said they didn't need anybody at the time. I proceeded to show them the garbage was piled to the moon, the windows were filthy, and the floors hadn't been really scrubbed good.

The guy looked at me and said, "You mean you'd start out in that area?" I said, "Hey, I'll start out in any area you'd like, to show you what I can do." At that point, he said, "Okay, show up tomorrow." So I started as a cleanup man.

Within three months they moved me to working foreman of the entire cleanup crew—and it was a large cleanup crew.

Then I moved into pasteurizing again. I had learned something about it when I worked at the dairy in Wenatchee. In Salt Lake I really got into it. With me, it's always been this way: I start out doing one job or one sport, and I get interested in another job or sport. So I'd always look to learn what the next thing was all about. So while I was a cleanup man, I would try to find out what was going on in pasteurizing, since being a cleanup man wasn't my idea of satisfaction.

I started talking to the guy who was doing by-products or something else to get an idea of what it was all about. I would actually stay over a couple extra hours sometimes to learn the different parts of the business. Then I started working in by-products part time helping the full-time guy. All of a sudden he got sick, and I asked the boss if I could take over. The supervisor said he and I would work it together. But after about an hour and a half the supervisor let me take it over myself.

Then I learned the entire pasteurization and homogenization processes, and eventually I was in charge of both by-products and pasteurization.

Still, this wasn't enough for me. I always have had plenty of energy and drive. All this while I was also working part time at a lumber-hardware store. I usually worked late hours at the dairy, like from eight at night until three in the morning. But I got out of school early, so I had free hours in the afternoon and was able to work at the lumber-hardware store too.

When I was nineteen and in about my third year of college, the money started to mean more to me because I got married—for the first time. A year later my first daughter—Robin—was born. I fathered five children altogether. And my second wife had two children by a previous marriage, so at one time I was supporting seven children. Now I'm married for the third time, to a girl named Melanie. We got married in the spring of '76, after we'd gone together for about two and a half years, and this one's for keeps. One thing we've promised ourselves for sure is: no kids!

Anyway, after I married my first wife in Salt Lake and we had our first child, it was more important to me to concentrate on making a living. I had the opportunity to become manager of the lumber-hardware store where I had been working, and also own a ten-percent share in the business. So I took it and quit school with about one semester to go. All along I had been majoring in physical education and business, figuring I'd end up in coaching. But once I got this chance to get into business and own a ten-percent share, I figured that's what I wanted to do. And I kept my hand in the dairy business too. One thing about me, I've never been too proud to do anything that needed doing. I'm forty-four now, but even now if things ever really got bad for me and Melanie, I could always get a job in a dairy or in the lumber business or in insurance or something else.

I managed the lumber-hardware store for four years, and I saved enough to open my own place. I had sold sporting goods along with the lumber and hardware at the other place, and my own store specialized in sporting goods. It was called Hiland Sports, like the name of the dairy.

Prior to that I had received a big disappointment when I had gone to the Olympic ski-jumping tryouts in 1960, at Iron Mountain, Michigan. I had kept active in the sport and thought I had a real shot at making the squad which would go to Squaw Valley, California. About fifty guys from all over the country came to the tryouts, a pretty large field.

I had never jumped on a big scaffold like they had at Iron Mountain and landed on ice. I had only jumped where you landed on snow. And the first time I walked up that scaffold to practice a jump I was holding onto the guardrail with both hands. It was the hardest thing in the world for me to shove off that thing with a big kick and come flying down. But it's amazing. Came time for the meet, it was the last thing I thought of. I charged up that thing without ever grabbing the rail, and I got up to the top and was really geared up. I was ready, as ready as I've ever been for anything in my life.

But about two-thirds of the way into my landing I lost control and when I came down, it was too short and I busted my ankle, and that finished me as far as the Olympics were concerned.

But I already had another sport I wanted to get into. It was parachuting. My first wife and I lived two blocks from the Salt Lake airport. I would be able to look out of our kitchen window and see these fellows jumping out of airplanes. The army parachuting team would demonstrate the sport in Salt Lake City all the time. I went over and talked to some people and got started doing it myself because it looked like real enjoyment. I gave somebody twenty-five dollars for immediate instruction, and pretty soon I got the hang of it.

With ski jumping I always hated to come down. I liked the sensation of flying. With the parachuting it was even better. I really love parachuting because as high as you go, as high as the plane goes, you can free-fall that much more. You could do back loops, forward loops, figure eights—anything that an airplane can do except go back up. Just a million things to do. Later on, when I got into national competitions with other experienced sky divers, we'd pass raw eggs back and forth and we'd chase each other all over the sky.

I hated to open. You're supposed to open at eighteen

hundred feet, and pretty soon you're stretching it to twelve hundred feet. A friend of mine and I used to do some screwy things. I filled his parachute with flour and turned around to watch him open. When he opened, boy! It was a big cloud. I was laying upside down laughing. Mind you, we're falling about two hundred and twenty feet a second, and I'm laughing my head off and still falling. I don't see the ground. I'm still laughing, saying, "Look at that!" And all of a sudden I turned over and said, "Oh, Christ, there's the ground!" That's one of the reasons I quit parachuting. I got so overconfident that many times I almost came right into the ground. I've opened as little as a hundred feet above the ground. I hit pretty hard. I broke my heels twice doing that. You're just having so damn much fun you just forget to open.

Of course, since I've always wanted to keep experiencing new things, after a thousand or so jumps in parachuting from planes I got so that I wanted to fly that plane. Eventually I started taking my own plane up and jumping out. I got my pilot's license and I bought my own plane. I even flew guys when their pilots weren't around, and I loaned my plane out too.

I competed in sky-diving events around the country for a few years. It's pretty much an amateur sport, but there are prizes and things to be won. Then, as kind of a side business, I opened a sky-diving center with a friend of mine. We rented out equipment and gave lessons and that sort of thing.

The same thing happened to me when I got interested in scuba diving. I really poured myself into it after someone introduced me to it. I read everything I could find by Jacques Cousteau and took lessons and all, and eventually I wound up giving instructions in it myself.

There's a funny story in how I got into cars from parachuting. There was a racetrack in Salt Lake City, the Salt Lake City Fairgrounds, and our parachuting team was invited to parachute into the middle of the racetrack one day as a demonstration and, I guess, an extra highlight for the fans attending the races. After we came down, we were guests of the track. We stayed and watched the races, and I got to stand inside and meet everybody there.

I always had had an interest in racing, even though I had never done any. Well, I couldn't believe the sensations I felt at the Salt Lake track. I found myself actually trying to push my foot through the ground—you know, imagining I was driving one of the cars myself. My hands were perspiring. I could feel the competitiveness of it. Right then and there I knew I had to drive a race car. It was as simple as that.

I went and bought an old junk heap for three hundred and fifty dollars. These cars were super-modifieds, like Indy sprint cars. They weren't terrific cars by any means, but the guy I bought that first three-hundred-and-fifty-dollar car from had built it in his garage out of pipe and that type of thing. I proceeded to crash it five times in a short time. Naturally, I didn't like what was happening. So I went to the bank and borrowed five thousand dollars and bought a new car, and the next year—that would have been 1965—I was the champion of the Intermountain Racing Association. We would race in Utah, Colorado, Idaho—places like that. It was pretty good racing. Some of the other drivers I competed against at that time were Jim Malloy, Billy Foster, and Art Pollard. All of them made it to the Indy 500, and unfortunately they're all dead now, killed in crashes.

The more I got into racing, the less my first wife liked it. She never had any objections when I was parachuting, no worries that I would get hurt, and since I wasn't spending a lot of money doing it, that was okay. But racing was taking some money, and she didn't like that. Security, the need for security, played a big part in my marital break-ups. My first wife and I split after twelve years. This was only a little while after I started racing. My second wife and I were married for seven years, and I was racing all that time. But security meant everything to her, and when we got a divorce after seven years she got everything.

Racing came fairly easy to me. From my other sports I was conditioned to be alert. In parachuting you have to land sometimes in little six-inch discs after coming down from ten thousand or twelve thousand feet. I used the same timing, skill, and coordination I developed in parachuting to advance myself in racing.

I was coming up in business at that time too. I sold my sporting-goods store and went to work for the Majestic Life Insurance Company in Salt Lake City in December 1965. It was a great job for my kind of schedule. I could work my own hours. I mostly sold insurance. In fact the first six months I was with Majestic I really devoted myself to it. In the first three months I sold one million dollars' worth of insurance each month. That's very, very good. Many guys are unable to sell one million dollars' worth in an entire year. The whole company had to expand because of all the business I brought in.

Just like in all the other businesses I've been in, my approach in insurance was motivation, mental attitude. People buy the person when you're dealing with a non-physical item, and I always made sure to emphasize this to the other men in the company.

I did so well they made me vice-president in charge of sales only a few months after I started with them. I was in charge of about fifty other guys. Some other companies were interested in hiring me. So I went in and asked the executives at Majestic about my future. That's when they made me vice-president of sales. By 1968 I was president of the company.

Majestic was part of a holding company called Omnico. Omnico got itself in a two-million-dollar dilemma. And in November 1969 the board of directors terminated the president and chairman of the board of Omnico and gave me the titles of chief executive officer, president, and chairman of the board.

Before that, though, in 1968 I took a leave of absence to concentrate on racing. I wanted to get into USAC racing. I contacted them, but they said I had too little experience in high-speed open-wheel competition. So I went

Dick Simon

159

to the Sports Car Club of America, and through extreme cooperation with that club I got them to waive a few rules and allow me in some races.

I got a borrowed Corvette and ran six races with it, winning two and finishing in the top three all six times. I got invited to the Race of Champions, the big event for sports-car club racing—amateur racing, more or less—at the end of the season in Riverside, California. I finished third in that.

This gave me the confidence I needed to go on. In '69, despite all the problems at the company, which required me to get involved in all kinds of decisions and meetings, I kept right on racing. I got a twelve-thousand-dollar second mortgage on my home and bought a used Lola and drove in six races with it. I won one and finished in the top six five times. With that record I went to USAC to see if they'd let me try Indy. They said to drive in two USAC races, and then they'd let me take their rookie test at the Speedway.

So I went to Phoenix, the last USAC race of the year, 1969, and proceeded to break the car. That meant I still needed two races for USAC. I was more determined than ever. Even though my business and wife needed me, I went and sold my personal assets like my boat, my motorcycle, my trailer, and a pickup truck to get enough money to keep myself racing. I was making forty to fifty thousand dollars a year in income as chief executive of Omnico, but that wasn't nearly enough for someone without sponsorship in USAC racing. So I had to sell a lot of stuff.

I set out in 1970, figuring this was the year I had to accomplish something. I went to a road race at Sears Point in California with a car I borrowed from Rolla Vollstedt, with whom I already had become friendly, and an engine from an old French car that had been driven in Grand Prix races. Against guys like A. J. Foyt, Mario Andretti, and other top names like that I finished sixth. Then we went to Phoenix, where they generally have a race early in the year and another one late. I qualified twenty-fourth and last on the grid but ended up sixth in the race.

The next race was at Trenton, and USAC suggested I go there too. It was the last race before Indianapolis, so I went there and took seventh.

That convinced USAC to let me take the rookie test at Indy. You have to understand this about the rookie test: Anyone who's never raced at Indy is considered a "rookie." This includes great champions from other types of racing. Grand Prix champions like Jim Clark and Graham Hill, when they came to Indianapolis, had to take the rookie test before they could try to actually qualify for the race.

I passed everything okay, and made the thirty-first starting spot in the field. I was really naïve then. I came to Indy figuring I could win. I didn't know about all of the things that could go wrong. I just charged forward. I had an engine that had already gone five hundred racing miles, which is just about the equivalent of one hundred thousand miles on your passenger car. So I went to Dan Gurney, from whom I had bought that engine, and said, "Sell me a better used engine, and I'll give you a post-dated check. I'm gonna win some money on race day." I hadn't even qualified yet, but Gurney believed in me and sold me another engine for eighteen thousand dollars. I went out and drove a strong race and finished fourteenth. It would have been higher, but the turbocharger gave us some trouble. For finishing fourteenth, I won eighteen thousand dollars, just what I needed to pay Gurney for the engine. So I made nothing out of the race, but we had gained some assets. Now I had a racing car and two engines.

Money certainly has not been the thing that's kept me in racing. I have yet to take ten cents out of racing. During all the years I owned my own car, anything I made in purses went back into the car. Between 1971 and '74 I was sponsored by TraveLodge Motels, but that wasn't really a big sponsorship, though a lot of people thought it was. The first three years they gave me fifty thousand dollars a year, and the fourth year one hundred thousand dollars. Rooms for the crew were also included.

But that's chicken feed when you consider that the Foyts, Unsers, Rutherfords, Andrettis, get hundreds of thousands of dollars in sponsorships every year, a hundred thousand dollars from this company and two hundred thousand dollars from that company. My deal was nothing compared to that, and in 1975 TraveLodge dropped out and left me with no sponsor.

I tried staying with Omnico as a consultant instead of chief executive, to give myself more time to devote to racing. But finally I terminated myself with the company. I had gone through my second divorce, and my wife got everything in that one. I figured as long as I had to start over again with a new life, I might as well do exactly what I wanted—which was racing. That's why I don't have much money today, but I'm enjoying myself more than I ever have. The people in racing—the drivers, the owners, all of 'em—they're the finest group of people I've ever been associated with. I want to win the 500 as much as anybody—probably more. The best I ever got was thirteenth place in 1972. I think we did great to get seventeenth place in 1976 after practicing for just seventeen laps. Most of our effort was devoted to getting Janet Guthrie's car ready. I'm no closer to winning now than I was when I first got to the Speedway in 1970. But that doesn't mean I'm ready to get out of it.

Hell, I only wish I had gotten into it ten years sooner. Maybe then I'd have a real chance. I know I can only keep going a few more years, maybe until I'm fifty. On the driving end of it, I mean. I'll stay in it in some capacity after I'm done driving. I'll be the first one to know when I can't race anymore. I'll come down into turn one at, say, 215 miles an hour, and I'll ease up a little more than usual. I'll realize it, and I'll say, "Oops, that's it. Time to go."

I'm a charger in racing, so other drivers will ask me to try out their car when they think something might be wrong. They know I'll let it all hang out for a few laps to see what goes on. I get out there and take the car to the point where the back end or the front end really slides. You can tell what's wrong with it that way. It helps the other driver, but it also helps me get exposure. People get to know what kind of guy I am.

I like challenges in life. I'm always looking for new ones. I guess I'll never stop looking. One of my big dreams is to dive off the Great Barrier Reef in Australia and look around underneath in my scuba gear. They say that the waters there are among the most beautiful you'll find anywhere—and also among the most dangerous for divers. But, hell, that's what makes it such a challenge for me, why I look forward to doing it someday.

Dick
Simon

163

johnny rutherford

JOHNNY RUTHERFORD is a leading name
among Indy drivers. But it took years to gain
that status.

I was born in Coffeyville, Kansas, on March 12, 1938, but in my early teens I came with my parents to Fort Worth, Texas, and I've been there ever since. I like the town very much.

At a young age I was successful in sprint and dirt racing, and many people expected me to be a big winner as far back as the early 1960s. The fact that it's taken me all these years to attain the level I'm at now has been frustrating. On the other hand, I feel I'm at an age now where I can better appreciate this success and can handle it better than I might have years ago. I'm not saying I would have preferred my career to go the way it has, but naturally I am very happy about the way things have turned out.

There's no set formula for success. Some people get the right breaks. My chance didn't come right away; it took a while. Let me give you an example of what I mean by getting a break early. Mario Andretti's a very good race driver, without a doubt one of the best in the business. But I remember a time when we were both young drivers—Mario's a couple of years younger than I am—and practicing before a race in Trenton, New Jersey.

Mario stuck his car in the fence, and Clint Brawner, one of the best mechanics around, said, "That kid oughta be banned from racing. He's a nuisance. He'll never make it. In fact, he'll be lucky to live through the summer."

A week later Brawner signed Mario, and you know where they went from there. Over the next few years Brawner was chief mechanic when Mario won a lot of big races, including the 1969 Indianapolis 500. Obviously, despite his negative statements about Mario that day in Trenton, Clint liked the way Mario always stood on the gas, and he figured he could use his own racing background and expertise to refine Mario's ability and make him a winning driver. All Mario needed, obviously, was for someone to stand on his neck on occasion. He had been driving too hard, but under Brawner, he quickly learned that if the car is right, you don't have to drive quite that hard.

The major point here is that Mario met up with a fellow like Brawner at an early age, and Brawner understood him and worked along with him. That doesn't often happen. I remember one car owner in California in 1962, when I was driving sprint cars in the International Motor Contest Association, a small racing circuit. He told me, "Kid, I don't think you're gonna make it." Since I had been doing very well on the IMCA sprint circuit at the time and was feeling pretty good about myself, that was the last thing I wanted to hear. But I didn't pay too much attention to him.

I guess I first realized I wanted to be a racedriver when I was ten years old. We were still living in Kansas at that time, and one day in 1948 my father took the family to see some midget racing at the fairgrounds in Tulsa, Oklahoma. After the feature race was over we went down to the pits and talked with some of the drivers. Right then and there, I told my father and mother this was the life I wanted to pursue.

I began collecting model cars and put together a lot of them from plastic kits. I was blessed with a fair amount of artistic ability, and I began drawing designs of racing cars. I also had some musical ability; I played the trumpet in grade school. But cars became an overwhelming interest of mine.

There was a very popular racing magazine at that time called *Speed Age,* and I read every issue avidly. I read about the great drivers of the late 1940s and early 1950s— men like Bill Vukovich, Troy Ruttman, Tony Bettenhausen, Marshall Teague, and Jimmy Bryan.

As I got older, I started participating in races myself. I remember a hot rod I had in my late teens; I fooled around with that for a while. In 1959, when I was twenty-one, I bought a '32 Chevrolet coupé that had been raced a lot—and also wrecked a lot. I fixed it up and took it racing at a place called Devil's Bowl Speedway in Dallas. I joined the Dallas Racing Club, and that was my start as a full-time racedriver.

When I said earlier you need a break to make it in racing, I didn't mean to suggest that I never received any. I had one very good break when I was just getting started—meeting up with Jim McElreath. Ten years older than I am, he had been running at the Devil's Bowl Speedway for a long time and doing very well. Jim was a bricklayer by trade, and he raced in order to make extra money. But many car owners who campaigned in the Midwest told him if ever he came up north, he should look them up. So in the spring of 1960 he went up to have a look, and I went along with him.

This gave me the opportunity to meet some nice people, and I got started driving the IMCA circuit on a regular basis shortly thereafter. As for McElreath, his decision to leave the Devil's Bowl Speedway also proved to be a wise one. He did very well on the Midwest tracks and eventually made it to Indianapolis. His biggest victory came when he won the first running of the Ontario five-hundred-mile race in 1970. He's still competing, and his son James also has taken up the sport now.

Anyway, I did very well with the IMCA sprint cars on the dirt tracks and built up a good reputation for myself as a short-track driver. By the middle of the 1962 season I managed to get a "conditional" license to drive USAC sprint cars, and at age twenty-four, I thought I was on my way. Some other people seemed to feel the same way about my career.

I went to the Indianapolis Motor Speedway for the first time in 1963. Driving a car owned by Eddie Kosteniuk, I qualified twenty-sixth and finished twenty-ninth in the race when I had to drop out with a broken transmission after forty-three laps.

1963 at Indy may not have been memorable from a racing point of view, but it certainly had its moments worth recalling. That's where I met Betty, my wife. I remember I was getting a push-off from the crew for the final laps of the driver's test all rookies at the Speedway have to take when I noticed this cute girl at the fence behind the pits. My antennae told me she seemed kind of, well, interested, so I winked at her. She winked back. Then to be certain the wink was intended for me, I waved at her. She waved back. Wouldn't you know that I'd go out right after that and spin like a top in the first lap? I doubt she was impressed.

But later that day I saw her again. I found out she was a registered nurse working at one of the Speedway first-aid stations, which then was located where the Goodyear tire shop is now. We started dating and were engaged one month later. We were married just two months after we met.

Aside from meeting Betty, probably the biggest thing that happened to me in 1963, my first full year of big-time racing, came in a stock car. At that time I was interested in stock cars and had gone to Daytona to drive for car builder Smokey Yunick, one of the major figures in stock-car circles. I drove his Chevrolet to a new track record. Later I won a hundred-mile Grand National qualifying race and finished ninth in the Daytona 500, which is the most important race on the National Association for Stock Car Auto Racing (NASCAR) schedule. This is stock-car racing's equivalent to the Indianapolis 500.

These successes were considered astonishing for a guy like me, who had never even driven stock cars before that year. However, I was much more interested in open-wheel racing and Indianapolis than a full-time ride in stock cars. I elected to proceed in that direction.

One valuable lesson I learned about that time was the necessity of staying in good shape. I'd always been on the thin side, but back then I weighed only one hundred and fifty-five pounds—I'm five-eleven in height—and I discovered that in the longer races I was having fatigue problems. In short races I was doing well, but in seventy-five and hundred-lap events at tracks like Salem and

Winchester in Indiana, I would literally be hanging out of the car by the fifty-lap mark.

I knew I'd have to do something, so I started working out and taking extra good care of myself. Pretty soon I had picked up ten pounds and was whizzing through those seventy-five-lappers. I always reflect on that period as the time when I not only got into good shape, but also picked up a hundred extra horsepower!

In 1964 I qualified for the fifteenth starting spot at Indianapolis. That was the year of a bad crash on the second lap, in which Eddie Sachs and Dave MacDonald were killed and a lot of other cars were wrecked. One of those wrecked machines was the one I was driving. Still, 1964 was a big year for me on the sprint-car circuit. I took fifth in the overall point standings and won a big feature race at Eldora Speedway in Rossburg, Ohio.

I was competing in the championship car events too, but I was bouncing around in several different cars. That's no way to develop any kind of record. Then, in 1965, I signed with a very good team—Bob Wilke and the Leader Card team, with A. J. Watson as the chief mechanic. I won the national sprint-car title that 1965 season. For the first time I won a championship race—a two-hundred-and-fifty-miler at Atlanta. I had more reason than ever to think that now I might really be on my way up the ladder.

I didn't figure—no one ever does—on a freak accident. It happened at Eldora Speedway in Rossburg. I had started the 1966 sprint-car season at Reading, Pennsylvania. This particular Sunday I was driving a new sprint car in the feature race. We were trying to sort it out, and I was running sixth or seventh in the pack.

Wally Meskowski, the car owner, saw that I was running high on the track and signaled for me to move down. I did, and Mario Andretti, who was driving another car owned by Meskowski, went by me. So I moved back up and was getting set to pass him back when his tire picked up a large clod of dirt or a rock—Eldora is notorious for rocks in the springtime—and it hit me right between the

eyes. Whack! Just like that. It certainly did gain my un-
divided attention.

Since we were running on a dirt track, my car then
hooked a rut and started flipping very violently out of the
race track. It went completely over the outside wall,
knocking me unconscious. Later on a doctor associated
with the NASA space program told me I had suffered *Johnny*
what astronauts call a redout, in which the head, from the *Rutherford*
upper lip all the way to the scalp, turns purple, like a big
bruise, because all the surface blood vessels have ruptured. *171*
In order for this to happen, you have to be pulling in
excess of ten negative G's. And, obviously, that's what had
happened when the car flipped over the wall.

Following that accident I spent three weeks in a Dayton
hospital and, over the course of the next eleven months,
underwent nine major operations on my right arm. I had
broken both arms in the crash and was required to wear
casts on both for three months, but the right arm had
been damaged more severely. It took a bone graft to
finally fix it properly. To this day I still can't straighten
my right arm to the full extension, which affects the way
I play tennis. Luckily I'm ambidextrous, so when I was
going through that frustrating period, I was able to use
my left arm—once it had healed enough—to eat and
carry on other normal activities.

Because of the accident I missed the 1966 Indianapolis
race and all of the rest of the season. In fact I didn't do
any racing again until Indianapolis in 1967. I probably
could have used a few races before that to work back
into it, but I already had missed one year at the Speedway
and didn't want to miss two years in a row.

Under the circumstances I was happy to qualify nineteenth in the 1967 race. But I lasted only one hundred
three of the two hundred laps and ended up in twenty-
fifth place. The rest of the racing season went pretty much
the same way—a down year.

I can't say I was surprised, really. After the accident at
Eldora, I had told my wife, Betty, that it would set me
back four or five years, and it turned out I was right. I

had seen it happen before. I had seen drivers go through serious situations and accidents, and it had taken them four or five years to get back.

It's a combination of mental and physical things. I was more ready to go mentally than I was physically, but it's a long process. And, remember, it's not just you, the driver, who's involved. You have to convince other people that you're able and ready to continue. Car owners—even some you've worked for before—aren't as apt to give you a ride as they were before. They say, "This guy's crashed very hard, and he may have lost it. I don't want to chance my car to him." It takes a while to get that kind of thinking straightened out and to convince people you actually are ready.

After the bad year in 1967, 1968 wasn't much better. For one thing, a few weeks before Indianapolis I had another accident, this one at Phoenix. I was in the dog-leg, really rolling, when Al Unser blew an engine. He kept moving, on into the pits. But here I come, running flat out, not aware of the trouble ahead. The steward hadn't thrown the black flag, indicating that Al's car was spilling oil. So I hit the oil full bore and my car spun into the fence.

Then along comes Roger McCluskey, who's leading the race. He hits the same oil, also spins, and hits me while I'm parked in the fence. Next it's Mario who's coming around. He's running second, turned on full, chasing McCluskey. He also hits the oil, spins, and clobbers both Roger and me. The side of my car was torn, the fuel tank opened up like a sardine can, and the fuel shot off sparks like a Roman candle. Before the safety crew could get me out, I suffered burns on my hands.

My hands had healed enough for me to make the Indy race, but on the one-hundred-twenty-fifth lap at the Speedway Mike Mosley and I spun to avoid Billy Vukovich's car, and I was hit from behind by my old Texas buddy, Jim McElreath, and the fuel tank in my car was punctured.

It was another sad story at Indianapolis in 1969. I

sprung an oil leak after twenty-four laps. The way my luck was going then, I'm sure that if I'd have owned any ducks, they'd all have drowned. Everything seemed to be in a state of limbo, and nothing seemed to go right. I was still feeling the effects of that first serious accident in 1966, and my feeling that it would take me four or five years to work back into serious contention in the sport was bearing out.

My luck began to change for the better in 1970, when I joined the Michner-Patrick Racing team. It was my first big breakthrough after several years of being on the outside looking in. I finished a disappointing eighteenth at Indy, but I qualified for the second starting spot, next to Al Unser, who not only won the pole but went on to win the race.

In 1971, again driving for the Patrick team, I qualified only twenty-fourth at Indy and managed to finish only eighteenth in the race. I qualified better in 1972—eighth—but finished worse, twenty-seventh. About that time I decided to leave the Patrick team. Things weren't going as well as I had hoped. Instead, I hooked up with Fred Gerhardt and the Thermo-King team. They had been looking for a new chauffeur and had a new car coming. Their previous driver, Jim Malloy of Denver, had been killed during practice at Indianapolis.

Before the new car was ready, I went to the Milwaukee race in one of Thermo-King's old cars. This proved not to be an especially fortunate move, because something broke and crashed me. The car caught fire, and I again got burned, so at that point I couldn't see how the change in teams was helping me at all.

But then we went to Pocono, the next race, and the new car, an Eagle, was ready. It was the first time I'd ever driven an Eagle, and it felt very good to bring it home second in the Pocono five-hundred-mile race, behind Joe Leonard.

Again, I said to myself, I'm on my way. And the rest of the year went fairly well. I didn't finish in the top three in any other races, but when the points were totaled up at the end of the season, I found myself in seventh place in the overall standings—the highest I had ever finished.

But then, that Thermo-King team started to crumble and fall apart. The chief mechanic left, and they didn't know quite what they were going to do. It was a very precarious and frustrating situation for me to be in.

So I decided to confide in an old friend of mine, Herb Porter, whom I have always felt free to talk with, that I really didn't know what I was going to do insofar as my future with Gerhardt and his team were concerned. Herb has been in and around racing for about forty years and is one of the greatest experts on racing engines who ever lived. He has been called the father of the turbocharger and has worked for Team McLaren as a consultant for some time.

When I told Herb of my problem, he pointed out that Team McLaren was looking for a driver to fill the seat vacated by Gordon Johncock, who had moved to another team. This was late in 1972, and I was tire-testing at Indianapolis. Herb told me that Teddy Mayer, the head of Team McLaren, was in the United States at that time, and that he might be able to arrange a meeting.

The next morning Teddy came to Indianapolis, and we had breakfast. That same afternoon I signed a contract. It was a great moment for me. I figured this was the best chance I'd ever have to get with a team that was first class all the way, a team that wanted to go racing as badly as I did. And they wanted somebody who had experience at the Speedway. So, looking back, you could say my signing with McLaren was the equivalent, finally, for me of the break Mario Andretti received from Clint Brawner way back in the early 1960s, when we both were young fledgling drivers.

Being with the McLaren people has been everything I could have hoped for. You can't do much better at Indianapolis than we did in our first four years together. Driving the Team McLaren cars, I had two firsts, a second place, and a ninth place. In 1973, my first year with Team McLaren, I won the pole at Indy with a record qualifying average speed of 198.413 miles per hour. Ironically, that was the year I finished ninth in the race, my worst in a McLaren car. I didn't even finish the race that year or in 1975, when I finished second. The only two times I've finished the 500 were in 1974 and 1976, both times in McLarens, and both times victories.

When I won in 1974, I came from the twenty-fifth start-ing spot. Ever since the 500 became an annual thirty-three-car affair in 1934, only one man had started further back than my ninth row, inside, position and won the race. That was Lou Meyer in 1936, who started twenty-eighth.

When I won Indy for the second time, in 1976, the race lasted only one hundred two laps, or two-hundred fifty-five miles, because of a severe rainstorm. The rules for the race say that if more than half has been run before it rains, the race is official. For a while the Speedway officials held off making the 1976 race official, in the hope that the rains would stop and that we could continue racing. But the rains never did let up, so the Indianapolis 500 of 1976 actually was the Indianapolis 255. It was the shortest race they ever had at Indy, though there had been rain-shortened races before.

I don't consider it any kind of fluke that I was in the lead at the time the race was stopped, and therefore adjudged the winner. I had been running in front the last twenty or twenty-five laps, so I feel I earned the vic-tory. In any event I'm not about to throw it back or ask for a recount.

The win at Indianapolis in '76 helped make up for the disappointment of not winning the national points cham-pionship. I never have won one, not even in 1974, when I won both the Indianapolis 500 and the Pocono 500, the only driver to win both the same year. In 1975 I came in second in the national standings, behind A. J. Foyt, but it was a distant second, 2,020 points behind. But going into the final race of the 1976 USAC championship season, a one-hundred-fifty-miler at Phoenix, I had a two-hundred-forty-point lead over Gordon Johncock, which appeared quite comfortable.

It meant that all I had to do was finish respectably high in the Phoenix race and I'd be the national champion. But the day turned out to be one of the most disappointing in my life. I hate those kind of races where you go in thinking you should be conservative and just drive hard enough to finish. Those seem to be the times when things go wrong, and that's exactly what happened this time. Some little two-dollar part went haywire and knocked us right out of the race. It was a fitting for the oil line, one of several new parts the crew had put on the car just so we could be sure of finishing.

Johncock ended up second in the race, making up all the points by which I had led him and then some. His final total for the season was twenty points better than mine, enough to give him the national championship.

The national title was something I had worked hard for all season, and to lose it in one race was a terrible setback. I feel this way about it, though—it gives me great incentive to go on and win that national title some other time. It's one of the big goals I have left in racing.

Still, it wouldn't be right for me to complain about the way things have gone for me. Of course, I am away from home an amazing amount of the time now, which is the way I knew it would be if I ever won Indianapolis. I always told my wife to be prepared for me to be away an awful lot if I ever did win it. But Betty's closely involved in racing herself and travels with me a great deal. She works with the team, keeping time and records at the races. Because of her closeness to the sport she knows how much it means to any driver to win the Indianapolis 500. It means, most of all, that you're virtually set for life, if you take advantage of it. And now that I've won it twice, all the good things we always had hoped for are happening to us.

I suppose our close family life is rather unique in racing. Very few of us have had the same wife for a great length of time. The younger or less mature drivers are liable to fall prey to the things that can happen to you in this sport or other sports. A driver wins the 500 or another major race, and suddenly his time becomes a problem. But in the case of Betty and me, I've always said that if we could persevere through the period when I would be away a lot—making promotional appearances, receiving this award or that trophy, or giving this or that speech—we would be broader and would benefit from it in the end. Right now I'm in that prime, and I am away a lot.

But we can handle it. Some drivers might not be able to. There are lots of women who avail themselves—or unveil themselves, as the case may be—to the men who are in racing. Some men might be more prone—no matter how I phrase this, it comes out sounding bad—or might get all gathered up in that sort of thing. He might go somewhere and he's lonely and soon someone's got him, and he changes his mind about the first one and goes off with the second one, and then his wife catches him or something else happens, and zap! there you go.

Betty and I have two children, Johnny IV and Angela, and they both have been racing now and like it, so I think we're a rather well-adjusted family. That's not always the case among racing families, or other sports.

The four of us traveled to Australia and New Zealand at the end of December 1976, and stayed for about three weeks into January 1977, and it was one of the most enjoyable experiences of our lives. We took lots of photographs that we'll always treasure, and it was a real highlight for all of us.

Another thing I feel sets me apart from some other drivers, aside from the close family ties, is the fact that I can get up in front of people and not stutter or stammer. I've always had this ability, and it's very important to me. I always felt being able to talk in front of an audience would help me project myself if and when the time ever came when people wanted to see and hear more of me. In a way I feel I was something of a success story waiting to happen, because I feel I had all the necessary attributes I needed to take advantage of success once it came.

One nice thing that's happened as a result of my articulateness and my easy way with words is the syndicated series of television programs I hosted, starting in the spring of 1977. Called "The Racers," the series covers all forms of motor sports—championship car racing, drag racing, unlimited hydroplanes, all that kind of thing. One show covers the 1976 Phoenix 150, the race in which I lost the national championship, as a portrayal of championship racing. As host of the series, I open and close each program and provide some commentary during the show. It's something I enjoy doing and of which I'd like to do more.

I've always told the younger drivers: Be prepared for the day when you can't do what you do best anymore. It's very important to look out for that day because if you don't plan where you're going when you're young, you're going to have some trouble later on finding the right thing to get into.

In my case I believe it was fortunate that I always had many interests. Even when I was first getting started in sprint-car racing and wasn't making much money at it, I was able to get home more than most drivers. The reason: I piloted my own plane to and from races. I had an Arco Commander 200, which I would fly into the Midwest for a race during the day, after which I'd fly back home the same night. Most of the small towns in the Midwest have airports which make flying back and forth very convenient. Now I own an old World War II fighter plane— a P-51—that is my pleasure for those few minutes I have away from racing.

I also still retain my boyhood interests in both art and music. I haven't had much time for painting in recent years, but I'm good with oils and pencil sketches and portraits. I did an oil portrait of Parnelli Jones that's hanging in the home of a friend of mine in California. Another oil I did of Don Branson is hanging in the USAC office in Indianapolis. Don was a fine driver who was killed in 1966, and I knew him well.

Another piece of art (a pencil sketching) I did was for Larry Truesdale, when he was the boss for Goodyear Tires. It shows A. J. Foyt in one corner, Bobby Unser in the other, and the Borg-Warner Trophy superimposed in the middle. The Borg-Warner is the trophy given each year to the winner of the Indianapolis 500. Another canvas I've done of my children isn't finished yet, but I intend to get to it one of these days.

As far as my music is concerned, though I played trumpet as a boy, I never did learn to read a note. But when it got out around Indianapolis a few years ago that I enjoyed music, they asked me to conduct the Indianapolis Symphony Orchestra one evening as a "guest conductor." My musical background and experience was written up in all the papers, but ninety-nine percent of that was all trumped up.

I always did have good rhythm, and can keep time well. So when I "conducted" the Indianapolis Symphony, all I really did was start them, stop them, and keep time in between. It wasn't particularly difficult to do. Just about anyone else could have done it as well as I did. But I really enjoyed it. I learned a lot about what goes on behind the scenes at a symphony.

Too many people tended to make a big deal of it. Many apparently got the notion I was a classical-music nut and that I played ninety instruments or something. But actually all I did was lead the Indianapolis Symphony in a rousing chorus of "Back Home Again in Indiana"!

About the full extent of my music now is the eight-track tapes I collect. I'm a fan of the big-band sound. I'm definitely not a rock music fan. Actually, I can't stand it. Both my children seem musically inclined, and they may be taking some sort of lessons soon.

The fact that I have interests like art and music seems odd to some people who are surprised that racedrivers like things like that. Part of the reason for this feeling is the fact that the racing clubs seem to fall down on the job of letting the public know about us as personalities. Each year racing acquires a lot of new fans, but they rarely hear about the kind of people we are, what interests we have, what we think, and how we feel. And I think these are things the racing public would like to know more about.

Of course, they also want to know as much as they can about the actual racing that goes on out on the tracks, and the biggest on-going story in championship racing is the speed. Everyone keeps hearing about the faster speeds that are coming at Indianapolis. When I set the record average speed while qualifying for the 1973 Indy 500, I didn't find it an especially scary ride, but at that speed, the margin for error is nil. We've seen some terrible crashes among drivers going at speed above 190. Art Pollard, for example, was going 192 in practice in 1973 when he crashed and was killed.

We ought to find a way to make competition, not speed. We could probably run 150 miles per hour and have everybody in the same lap racing each other, and that would be more exciting than two cars running 190 and everybody else running 175 or 180.

Having said that, I still feel we'll see 200-mile-per-hour qualifying speeds at Indianapolis in 1977. The cars are more efficient than ever. The engines have more horsepower, and they work better. Even with all the restrictions racing officials have put in to try to reduce the speeds, the speeds keep increasing anyway. You can credit good old ingenuity for that.

I don't think the rules restricting speeds make much sense the way they're presently constituted. They actually only limit the speeds the cars can run during the race. The variations between the qualifying speeds and the race speeds have become so great it's a farce. What I'd like to see is not so much of a gap between them.

A lot of drivers have expressed the opinion that we should go slower. Some people outside of racing think we're afraid to speak up on this subject, because it's not the *macho* thing to do. But many guys have spoken out about the speeds, including me, and we're quite serious about it. But there's very little we can do about it. We're hired on to drive the cars.

The problem comes, I believe, from the fact that very few drivers—maybe only a handful—are capable of running 200 miles an hour. There are some guys who ought to be limited to 55 miles an hour, but the guy who shouldn't even be going 55 is going to be asked to go 200 someday, and that's when trouble starts.

You might think higher speeds would weed out the less competent drivers, but the way it usually happens is like this: A mechanic gets itchy and turns the wick up because he wants to make the car go better. A lot of times he'll make it go better than the driver can safely handle. Looking at it another way, if the driver makes it, he's got the experience at the higher speeds, and they haven't hurt him a bit. Maybe in a way it all works out.

The big challenge in auto racing is posed in this question: Can human progress keep pace with mechanical progress? I don't think anyone really knows the answer, but like everyone else, I'm anxious to find out. Whether you're a competitor or just a fan, that question makes the sport so very interesting.

Johnny Rutherford

181